Memory
Makes
Money

Memory Makes Money

by

HARRY LORAYNE

Little, Brown and Company
Boston · Toronto · London

FIRST EDITION

Artwork by Robert E. Lorayne

Library of Congress Cataloging-in-Publication Data

Lorayne, Harry.
  Memory makes money.

  1. Mnemonics. 2. Memory. 3. Business — Psychological aspects. 4. Executives — Psychology. I. Title.
BF385.L7553 1988   153.1'4   88-9494
ISBN 0-316-53267-3

10 9 8 7 6 5 4 3 2 1

RRD-VA

Designed by Jacques Chazaud

Published simultaneously in Canada
by Little, Brown & Company (Canada) Limited

PRINTED IN THE UNITED STATES OF AMERICA

For Renée and Robert

There can be no better memories
than those they've given me

Contents

Acknowledgments

My thanks to all of the following — none of whom I'll ever forget:

My editor, Fredrica S. Friedman, who made me sound better than I really do; Frank V. AtLee; Phyllis Barr; Evan R. Bell; Philip A. Bossert; Mel Brooks; Joseph V. Casale; Edmond E. Chapus; A. S. Clausi; Steven A. Conner; Ralph Destino; Gerald S. Deutsch; Alan Greenberg; J. K. Hartman; Ellen Hassman; George J. Konogeris; Peter Kougasian; Arlie Lazarus; Harvey Leeds; Cy Leslie; Arthur Levitt, Jr.; Dr. Sheldon Lippman; Saundra Malvin; Dr. Jesse Manlapaz; Scott Marcus; Ruth Mass; Charles Nelson Reilly; Stephen Rose; Richard Roth, Jr.; Vincent Sardi; Richard Schlott; William Seco; Bernadette Skubly-Butts; Victor Sperandeo; Michael K. Stanton; Luna Carne-Ross; Lois de la Haba; Debbie Roth; Michael Brandon; and, of course, my wife, Renée.

It is not enough to have a good mind. The main thing is to use it well.

— RENÉ DESCARTES, *Les Discours de la Méthode*

Memory
Makes
Money

1
The
Memory-Handicapped

Every writer looks for a *hook*. A hook with which to grab the reader, and make him or her continue reading. I want you to continue reading, perhaps even buy this book if you're browsing in a bookstore. So, here's my hook:

I'm going to make you hate me!

That should make you continue reading, because I'm sure you want to know *how* I'm going to make you hate me.

You're going to dislike me because I'll berate you for not taking advantage of — for not *using* — the greatest God-given ability possessed by man: the ability to *remember*, to use your *memory*. You'll dislike me for telling you that you don't *do* what you already *know* how to do, or already can do — that is, *use* your memory. We all have great memories — but I know how to use mine, and I *do*. You *don't*. Many use their supposedly bad memories as an excuse, an excuse for not producing at peak efficiency. That's a cop-out. I'll teach you to close that gap between "knowing" and "doing." Then you'll be able to stop pretending that you can't remember (and, also, stop pretending that you're not pretending)! I'll make you think a bit *differently,* get you out of the thinking rut, and I'll do it without causing you any pain. You might even enjoy it. If you like to see results, as I do, I *guarantee* you'll enjoy it.

You may think you have an adequate memory now. The problem is that memorizing or learning data by rote is a drudgery and a bore — so you usually rely on notes. I guarantee to take that drudgery out of learning/memorizing. Not only will you remember anything you want to in a fraction of the time it now takes you, but it will be imaginative and fun to do.

A great memory gives you the *edge* you need in business. The more you *impress,* the more of an edge you'll have, and the more business you'll do. Just try to visualize the impression you'll make when you can quote prices, style numbers, premiums, and interest rates (*facts*) without referring to lists; accomplish every one of your daily errands and chores and keep every one of your business appointments without ever searching through pockets or purse for lists or schedules; deliver sales talks or speeches or business reports while making eye contact with your audience because you don't have to look down at notes; recognize the face and *know* the name of all your clients; remember corporate affiliations easily; never waste time and money searching for misplaced files, letters, memos — and much more.

It boils down to being *noticed*. Most of your business counterparts probably have basically the same skills and education that you do. Acquiring the incredible, computerlike, steel-trap mind the systems in this book will enable you to acquire will set you apart, put you in command. You will have utmost confidence in yourself, because you *know* you know all the data. Confidence exudes power, and power and recognition are what it's all about — because they lead to *making money!*

Yes, that's the edge *everyone* is searching for. In an article about the drug industry, *Fortune* magazine said, "Next to new cancer therapies, the quest for memory-improving drugs is the hottest area of medical research."

Most books on how to succeed in business offer *general* advice. They make you nod your head, and think, "Gee, that sounds good." But that's usually it; they don't really *teach* anything. I'm much too result-oriented for that, and so are the many corporations that make sure my methods are taught in their training programs. They're not about to spend big bucks for *theory;* they want (and get) *results.*

That's what you're offered here. When you have more knowledge than others in your business, which means you *remember* more about the business — more facts, more detail, more *data* — you are the one with that extra *edge.* Apply the systems I'll teach you and you will acquire perhaps the *most* useful, concrete, and essential business/management tool.

Give yourself that business edge! As Raymond C. Johnson, former Vice Chairman of New York Life Insurance Company, pointed out: "It takes just a little more than ordinary effort to move ahead of the herd. We do not achieve success by being *twice* as good as the other fellow. The moment a person adds *just a little extra,* his accomplishments and his income increase in geometric proportions."

You'll be amazed at how much more than "just a little extra" you can add when you apply my trained-memory systems — and you'll add it with just *ordinary* effort.

Would you hire someone who was always bumping into desks and other people, knocking over computers, or crashing into the water cooler because he didn't see well and refused to be fitted for glasses? Or someone who continually said, "Sorry, what was that?" or "Speak louder, please," all because she refused to wear a hearing aid?

I don't think so. Few people in the business world would put themselves at such a disadvantage when it wasn't necessary. Of course, we hire the handicapped. But not someone who handicaps himself deliberately.

The point? Why hire — or why not fire — someone who is *memory-handicapped* when he or she doesn't have to be? And, there's no need for *you* to be one of the memory-handicapped. Believe this: It is easier and more fun and cheaper to acquire a fantastic memory than it is to be fitted for eyeglasses or a hearing aid!

There is, always has been, a wide gap that needs filling in business. We live in an era often referred to as the age of the information explosion. And that flood of data shows no sign of lessening; as a matter of fact, it is *accelerating*. Besides the obvious data that business people have to remember — like names and faces of clients and potential clients, style numbers, telephone numbers, names of places and products, and so forth — think of how businesses have *expanded*. Automobile companies used to put out one car each year. Now they put out numerous models each year. Your bank offered a savings account and a checking account years ago. Today you can choose from among perhaps twenty different kinds of accounts. Think of all the new data involved — the additional knowledge needed to service clients in these and practically all other business areas. Technology and data keep coming. Somebody has to remember some of that data: *You* do!

That's the memory gap, and the time has come to fill that gap for yourself. You are *not* locked into the lousy memory with which you were born. Double fallacy there; you *weren't* born with a lousy memory. You have a great memory right now — just try forgetting something you already know! And — check this out with any trial lawyer — when the judge instructs the jury to disregard (forget) a remark just made, they remember it better, longer, and more clearly than most of the other testimony.

Have I impressed upon you the importance of memory in business? If not, let's see if **Arthur Levitt, Jr.,** Chairman of the American Stock Exchange, can:

> All kinds of negotiations take place when one runs an exchange — negotiations with contractors in the construction of facilities, negotiations with firms in pricing various services — so if you've forgotten various ingredients that go into those negotiations, it can be very costly to you.
>
> I think also that it's a highly political environment. We

constantly depend upon the assistance of Congress and the Securities and Exchange Commission. To forget what has been agreed upon in those areas, in the political arena, can be extraordinarily costly, not so much from a dollar-and-cents point of view as from a practical business point of view.

Also, if you forget that you've given a waiver to a particular listed company to do something, that can be extremely costly in terms of your credibility. I think that's the major issue. So much of this business depends upon one's word, one's bond, one's integrity, that the line between forgetting and misleading is a very narrow one, and the danger you run into by forgetting pledges, commitments, agreements, understandings, is that your credibility would be impaired. That would be a critical failing for people who operate in this world which depends so much upon personal word, personal bond.

Arthur Levitt obviously places high priority on remembering — or on not forgetting, if you prefer. So does every executive I interviewed for this book. When I asked where the importance of memory should be rated on a scale of 1 to 10, I received mostly 10's and 9's. *No one* thought it rated below 8. Think about your business, your position, or the position you'd like to reach in the corporate world. Think of all that you have to learn, know, remember. Where would *you* rate the importance of memory on the 1-to-10 scale?

Cy Leslie *(Chairman and CEO, MGM/UA Home Entertainment Group):* A successful business person doesn't want to relearn, relive, reinvent wheels. The knowledge I had — what I remembered from the mass-market recording business I started — enabled me to start the business I'm in now, in which I make much more money. The techniques of marketing merchandise and the interrelationship with people are no different. In my opinion, remembering is the key to success — because the fact is, where we succeed or where we fail is a product of memory.

Scott Marcus *(President, Evan-Picone Shoes, division of U.S. Shoe Corporation):* I find "I forgot" to be an irresponsible answer for a professional businessman to give. I think a professional doesn't forget. Our salesmen are always presenting the tangible shoe. They can refer to a book at any time, but it certainly aids their ability to sell if they remember the style name and/or number, as well as the material that the shoe is made of, its heel height, and so forth. When dealing with buyers, the salespeople must remember these things in order to talk about the shoe — in order to *sell* it. The names and styles change seasonally, so it's a continual memory problem. Those who remember all the data *always* sell better, sell more — and therefore make more money.

Memory is the key enhancing factor to someone's career.

2

Learn from Top Money-Makers

A Super Memory Gives You an Invaluable Edge in Your Business or Profession

Recently I personally conducted a poll of corporate CEOs (chief executive officers), which included some of the top people I interviewed for this book. It showed virtually the same results as a poll I conducted for an article in *Nation's Business* magazine some years ago. One of my questions was "How important is a good memory in your business?" Eighty-five percent in the new poll answered that a good memory is "essential" in their businesses. The remaining 15 percent of the responses were divided among "important" and "very important." *No one* checked off the "not important" box. The interesting, and only, change is that a higher percentage answered "essential" in the more recent poll.

Frank V. AtLee *(Executive Vice President, American Cyanamid Corporation):* If you have a poor memory, you just can't keep up with the work. An executive needs a system to help him remember.

In order to compete and survive in today's business world, the executive (and the person striving to reach executive level) needs not only the hide of an elephant, but the proverbial *memory* of an elephant as well.

CEOs and COOs (chief operating officers) don't want their managers spending hours searching for their eyeglasses (which are probably perched on their heads). Not on company time. Multiply a thousand managers each searching for his or her glasses — or pens, appointment books, telephone numbers — for an hour, and that's one thousand hours (that *day*). That costs money!

Memory is time is money. So, one of the techniques taught in this book will enable the manager/executive to eliminate all the absent-mindedness that costs — *wastes* — time at the office. And — **Memory instills confidence, which creates sales.** Suppose that you're sitting opposite a potential client trying to sell him an insurance policy. After you've talked for some time, he says, "Oh, I want my seventeen-year-old daughter to be covered, too. How much more will the premium be?" You can say, "Okay, let me check," and search through your rate book (the insurance agent's bible) for the answer — finding it after anywhere from one minute to half an hour.

Or . . . you can answer, "Good idea. It would cost you another $18.75 per quarter to cover her up to age twenty-one." You *know* that because you've applied my trained-memory systems. You can give the answer immediately. That instills in your client a confidence in your abilities. That impresses. That, very likely, will clinch the sale. And —

Memory makes *you* memorable. In our competitive world, just about all products and services are comparable. So you've got to sell *yourself* before you can sell your particular product or service. Calling a prospective client "Paul" when his name is Sam is not the way to sell yourself. If Sam has a choice, he's going to give his order to the salesperson or executive who calls him Sam — not "Paul," or "Captain," or "Buddy," or "Sweetheart," or "Darling." The ability to remember people and facts about them has obvious practical benefits in business — it brings in business.

A management group that works for you and *with* you offers a huge personality plus. In this computerized age of big business, of *impersonal* business, it's a strength to make your people feel as if they're part of a *family*. What better way to make them feel that way than to remember/know details about *their* families. Check any statistics you like — the companies whose people consider themselves a part of a "family" are the more productive, excellent companies. And by remembering subordinates and clients and facts about them, *you* will be remembered. When you're remembered, more business — more money — *must* come your way.

A little edge can make an awfully big difference. Successful people are not necessarily smarter than nonsuccessful people. They simply use what we all have more effectively. They have the same memory: there are only trained and untrained memories. Train *your* memory, and you'll acquire that edge.

You probably invest a large chunk of your time and effort into career, profession, position. I can make it so much easier for you — free up so much of that time for you. Because, with your newfound ability to remember, you will accomplish more in less time than you ever dreamed possible.

Dr. Jesse Manlapaz *(Neurosurgeon, Danbury Hospital, Danbury, Connecticut):* Without memory I'd lose every patient. When I'm doing brain surgery, I have to *remember* everything in order to *know* what I'm doing.

And, Mr. or Ms. Executive, you don't think twice about getting help in any and all "acceptable" areas. You'll go to a golf pro to learn how to swing a golf club and you'll get help from a tennis pro. But society has taught you — told you since your school days — that the memory you're born with is *it;* that when you reach adulthood, you also reach the limit of your mental capacity, the limit of your memory capacity. Well, that simply isn't so. Robert Frost would have told you it isn't so, as would Pablo Casals, Georgia O'Keeffe, and Carl Sandburg. George Burns and Helen Hayes will tell you it isn't so.

These are only a few who did or do some of their best work, and had or have great functioning memories, in their eighties and nineties.

You can train your memory to work at peak efficiency no matter what your age. And it's easier to learn to remember to a fantastic degree than it is to learn to swing a golf club correctly.

Scott Marcus *(President, Evan-Picone Shoes, division of U.S. Shoe Corporation):* A good memory has *always* been essential in business — from sales to management to running divisions to running companies. Memory keeps me in control of my business.

In business, the thinking on the subject of memory has changed. Years ago, when I wanted to get my systems into corporate/industrial training programs, I arranged an interview with the CEO of a large manufacturing company. I talked about how great my memory techniques were, and what a good teacher I was. The CEO listened, but not with rapt attention; a sheer curtain had dropped over his eyes. When I finished, here's what happened (it changed my life, career-wise):

He picked up an ashtray, held it up in front of my nose, and said, "Harry, it cost me one dollar to make this ashtray. How can you help me sell it for a dollar and a half?" The point: profit — *money* — is what interested him, and that's where I had to grab him. I didn't (and don't) know anything about the manufacturing or the selling of ashtrays, but I'm pretty good when my back is against the wall. So I asked, "How much do you spend training your personnel each year — ballpark?" He answered, "About a million dollars." I said, "Don't you realize that about 75 percent of what you're teaching your people is *forgotten?* That means that $750,000 a year is going right into the porcelain file!" The instant I mentioned losing $750,000, the curtain lifted; I had his undivided attention.

"Let me teach your people how to remember *first,* before you put them through any other training. Then, they'll remember everything they're being taught — and you've saved $750,000!" *That* he understood. And *that* is what got me involved in the corporate area — because what I made up on the spur of a panicky moment ended up being true.

I no longer have to prove anything; business people are aware of the importance of memory. As **Philip A. Bossert** — Director of Sales, Advertising, and Publicity for *Business Week* — said to me, "Memory? You're dead if you don't have it!" We're talking about *profitable* memory power. "Money" memory. Oh yes, business is aware of the importance of a high MQ — memory quotient.

Victor Sperandeo *(Managing General Partner, Hugo Securities Company):* Once a person has the desire to succeed, he or she has to memorize (learn) everything he can about his business. . . . People must know how to memorize large quantities of information, to program their minds as they program a computer. . . . And how to make remembering fun. (I'm a good example of your teachings; you're my guru, Harry.)

Ruth Mass *(President and Owner, Humbert Travel, one of the larger U.S. travel agencies):* Everything is memory! My business revolves around memory and remembering — we're using our memories every single minute of every business day. I have to remember who to call at what telephone number in order to get specific information fast, what code to feed into the computer, who's the sales representative for which airline, fares, airports, charters, clients' names and telephone numbers and travel preferences — it's *all* memory.

The executives I interviewed for this book represent many areas of the business/corporate world, and range from account executives to partners, to vice presidents, to presidents, to chairmen of the board. They will help me impress upon you just how important — essential, critical, urgent, crucial, vital (I'm using some of their adjectives) — a good memory is in every business area.

Michael K. Stanton *(Partner, Weil, Gotshal and Manges, among the top twenty law firms):* Memory is critical; you'd *better* remember the facts of your case. You've got one shot in front of the judge — that's opening *and* closing night.

And philosopher William James said, in an essay on the subject of memory, "The man whose acquisitions stick is the man who is always achieving and advancing, whilst his neighbors, spending most of their time in relearning what they once knew but have forgotten, simply hold their own."

Your capacity to remember and *retain* data (and, of course, to use that data) sets the level of achievement in your business and professional life. Applying the systems and techniques taught in this book will greatly increase your learning capacity. And, as most top executives agree, *learning* capacity has a direct relationship and effect on *earning* capacity.

Philip A. Bossert *(Director of Sales, Advertising and Publicity, Business Week):* I think that remembering well is the mark of a professional; the fear of a professional is forgetting. The fear is that people will think you're not interested if you forget. Interest level is measured by how much you remember.

Ralph Destino *(Chairman, Cartier, Inc.):* You know what's interesting here, Harry? Someone has got to say how important and vital an outstanding memory is to business success — that a great memory distinguishes you immediately, makes you *noticeable*. Harvard Business School doesn't say it — *you* are saying it!

3

An Interview with Mel Brooks, CEO

In preparing this book, I interviewed many executives at length on the role memory plays in business. I'm including only two of these interviews in virtual entirety. I chose these two because both of the subjects come from humble beginnings and are now very successful, and because their words are representative of the general business tone and spirit I felt during all my interviews.

Most people think of **Mel Brooks** as an outrageously funny man. He is that. He is also an astute and brilliant businessman, the President and CEO of Brooksfilms, Inc. (producers of such goodies as *The Elephant Man, Frances, The Fly,* and *84 Charing Cross Road*). I sat Mel down (not an easy feat) and turned on the tape recorder. The interview reveals a little bit of both sides of this extremely talented person. Read, learn, enjoy.

HL: Do you feel you're different from most people?

MB: I'm shorter! And I'm more Jewish than — Jews. My nose and my accent — you know — there's a lot of things that make me unique.

HL: I'm short, too — you're not that different.

MB: I always have something hanging out of my nose.

HL: *That's* unique.

MB: Well, three-year-olds often do too, but for somebody in his late fifties to have something hanging out of his nose — yeah, that's unique.

HL: Is it important to have the facts in mind when discussing a business deal? No notes?

MB: Absolutely. Without those facts in mind, I'm not going to do well. It's like working on stage or in the movies. I rehearse a little and remember significant details to help me make the deal. If the meeting is in my office, I can have the fact sheet on my desk. Where *you* have been a great help to me is when the meeting is elsewhere; I can't sneak a look at a piece of paper then. And I gotta seem like I'm knowledgeable, like I've done my homework, like I *care*.

HL: Why do you think that's important, Mel?

MB: You're trying to raise between 60 and 100 million dollars for ten movies. You're meeting with money people. They don't want to see you looking down at something; they like you to have facts at your fingertips. That's *very* important.

HL: You're not only a businessman; you're one of our comic geniuses. Is memory involved? Do you have to remember what came before in comedy?

MB: It's critical to remember what came before. I go back to the Joe Miller joke books to know what something is based on. So that I don't repeat, and so that I know it's rooted in something good. And, when I'm doing the Carson show, I can't look at idiot cards, I can't read — that's bad. They *see* your eyes moving on a close-up. I've got to listen backstage and hear what Johnny is saying, and remember it — so I can refer to it later, make fun of him, make fun of the previous guest. I've trained myself to grasp significant clues to help me remember the sentence, the paragraph, the story or concept.

HL: Mel, how would someone move up in your organization?

MB: He or she would have to have an overview of Brooksfilms, of course. And I try to have people who can give me fountains of information when and where I need it. Either by having remembered it or by having done the right research. For a movie, we sometimes do a year of research. I need people who can retrieve information, among other things.

HL: Is there one person whom you depend on more than others?

MB: Yes. Leah Zappy. She's been with me for eleven years, and she knows where the key to the toilet is! She just made me $16,000 in a minute by remembering — by *remembering* — to check with NBC about my show *Get Smart*. My accountants didn't remember to check. And when you have a piece of a syndicated show, the broadcasting companies don't always automatically send moneys that come due. A little *reminder* is sometimes necessary.

HL: And do you lose faith in people who use "I forgot" as an excuse?

MB: I've fired people who consistently said "I forgot," because that's a very bad bottleneck and stumbling block. "I forgot" is no excuse. "I forgot" once — maybe, but "I forgot" three times? And where it's critical? And if it costs the company money (which it usually does)? No way.

I met a kid named Arthur Levitt III. He's the assistant to Michael Eisner, who runs Disney. Michael met Arthur when Arthur was selling furniture. Michael was so impressed with the kid's knowledge of the catalog that he hired him. Of course he has a good personality too. But a good and efficient business personality is nothing without memory. Memory is the cornerstone that it stands on. It helps you *build* that personality.

I need people who can give me answers in a fraction of a second. Time is money. I'm on a set, and somebody says, "You need this-and-this shot," and Ezra Zwerdlow, my coproducer says, "No, you have that shot, Mel; I remember that you shot it as a close-up. Someone lost it." It *was* lost in the editing room. We both remembered we had made the shot. The script supervisor had forgotten to list it. It saved an awful lot of money and time, because we *remembered*.

HL: Do you think you could have reached your position if you didn't have such a good memory?

MB: It's critical. It's critical. The most difficult thing I do is learn character lines. But I remember when you were working with Annie [actress Anne Bancroft, Brooks's wife] and she had a particularly difficult play to do, a Bill Gibson play — *John and Abigail*. And there were no cues. The two actors couldn't cue each other. That's important, because when an actor gives you a line, you can return it. But these were non-sequitur letters; there were no cues, no continuity. I was there when you helped her with one line.

HL: There were many. The one you mean wasn't that tough. The line was ". . . whether the soldiers cross the bridge." Annie kept saying, ". . . *if* the soldiers cross the bridge," during rehearsals. She said to me, "Harry, for God's sake, how do I remember that it's not 'if' "? I asked, "What's the first thing that comes to mind when you think 'whether' "? Annie said, "Snowstorm!" (She thought "weather.") I said, "Fine, visualize the soldiers crossing that bridge in a snowstorm." That did it. Once she "saw" that image, she always said "whether," not "if."

MB: I took a page from your book; when I study lines, I always visualize "pictures" because without them the lines just won't stay in my head.

HL: So, on a scale of 1 to 10, where would you rate the importance of memory?

MB: It's a 28! For the CEO of a company, it's essential. For an actor, it's critical. It's $92,000 a day — you can't forget lines! Besides, if you're not on top of your lines, something's wrong with your eyes, something's wrong with the tone of your voice, something's wrong with the rhythm of your performance. It *shows*. I can't afford to have actors forget lines. Costs too much money. I tell my actors to read me their parts — without looking at idiot cards. They must *know* their lines; that's part of my contract. Not approximately, *exactly*. I'm also proud of the words I've written; I don't want anyone changing them.

HL: I enjoyed helping you and Annie remember the Polish lyrics to "Sweet Georgia Brown" for your movie *To Be or Not to Be.*

MB: Absolutely. We couldn't have done it without you. It was like charades — you helped us break it down into sounds, textures, meaningful pictures.

HL: The way it was shot, you couldn't look at idiot cards.

MB: No. So we did what you taught us. We visualized pictures for each sound. Much easier than trying to remember foreign sounds by rote.

HL: Mel, give me one instance where forgetting cost you money.

MB: I forgot the bottom line on a price and came in too high for the movie rights to a property. An agent had mentioned to me that $62,000 was the bottom line, and would have bought it. I forgot that — and bid $110,000. The property was *The Elephant Man.* It turned out all right, but I could have saved the $48,000 if I had remembered that one piece of information.

HL: And an example where remembering something *helped?*

MB: Yes, definitely. My first deal with Alan Ladd, Jr. — I remembered some of the obscure pictures his father (Alan Ladd) had made, and it warmed the cockles of his heart. Because of that we got along. He loved me, and he took *Young Frankenstein* away from Columbia Pictures. He didn't love me *only* because of that, but it sure helped. Most would remember *Shane,* but I remembered that Alan was in *The Goldwyn Follies,* that he was a tenor, and had about a minute in that film. Alan Ladd, Jr., was thrilled. He said I was the only one who remembered that. It won big points for me. By the way, Alan Ladd, Jr., and I have gone from *Young Frankenstein* to *Silent Movie* to *High Anxiety,* and now [at the time of this interview] we're doing *Spaceballs.* So it was critical for me to win him over.

HL: If you could make your memory utterly fantastic in one area, which would you select?

MB: Good question. I would chose to remember facts and figures — actors' prices, films' earnings. To have those facts at my fingertips when I'm selling, convincing. To quote correct prices. It's very important. What a car costs, I don't care — but I have to apply your systems to help me remember lines, and business figures. If a picture did over $100 million, I've got to know it. For instance, when I offered one director [David Cronenberg] more than he had asked, he was flabbergasted. I knew he was worth it. He asked for an amount. I said, "That's the wrong figure." He was ready to walk, and I said, "I'm giving you $250,000 *more* than that!" You see, I knew/remembered his track record. I knew exactly what he'd done at the box office.

If I hadn't remembered those box-office figures, I wouldn't have known his true worth and I wouldn't have offered that much — and I might have lost him. The movie I hired him for was *The Fly*. It turned out to be a $100-million movie. And for an extra couple of hundred thousand dollars, I had secured the services of a genius with a box-office track record.

HL: Well, Mel, what have I not asked that I should have asked?

MB: You haven't asked me if I love you!

HL: No, I mean in the area of memory, and money — money is the key here.

MB: Yes. What you should stress is the fact that when you have knowledge at your fingertips you multiply your worth, you multiply your value. When you *don't* have that knowledge, when you're "vamping till ready," it's apparent. And what we who run companies do is — we're very polite, but we say "good-bye," and never see that person again. Arthur Levitt III remembered everything in that catalog; he quoted prices without checking. Because of that he is now a vice-president at Disney, and doing a great job, and if I could steal him, I would. So, I'm telling you, knowledge is power, and memory *does* make money! Memory is the critical ability to retrieve knowledge. You fail or succeed by your retrieval capabilities.

HL: Mel, you're a terrific person.

MB: Well, I love you, too, Harry. Because your methodology has helped me to be more successful. You also make me laugh and lend me money!

HL: Annie once wrote to me, saying, in part — "I want to thank you for making the drudgery [learning scripts] part of my creative art.''

MB: Yes, I know. We both use your methodology for that. We do exactly what you taught us to do. We make pictures in our minds, and *see* them, insane ones — sometimes we see Picassos in our heads. That's not bad!

HL: As long as it works.

MB: Exactly. And it sure does.

HL: Is memory important in business?

A. S. Clausi *(Senior Vice President, General Foods Corporation):* It's very, very important; in fact, it's critical. Obviously, remembering as much information about your business as possible is important. In my particular area of research, aside from remembering basic office procedures, I need to remember *past* research. I have to remember the research I'm involved in at the present time — which steps have been taken and which haven't — and I want to remember the research yet to be done. It's a continual memory situation. Things can be looked up, but that takes time. It's better to remember them. In fact, that's precisely what we do — remember most of the material. It becomes part of our "fabric."

HL: Would you say that you and others at your level became the senior executives you are *because* you remember more than others — more than those who have not reached that level, those who always have to look things up?

ASC: I like to think I became the successful executive I am because of a whole range of things, a very important part of which is my memory.

4

How Good Is
Your Business
Memory?

---

*Test Your Memory
in Twelve Important Business Situations*

I asked the same questions of most of the executives I interviewed for this book. One was "What would make you *notice* someone in your employ? What would make him or her stand out?" Most of the answers contained the word *results*.

To **A. S. Clausi,** Senior Vice President of General Foods Corporation, I said, "I have a silly question: How often would you put up with, if at all, the excuse 'I forgot'?" His answer:

No, it's not a silly question. I wouldn't put up with it very often from any one employee. I think you'd get the same response from any of my peers, no matter which department. Generally, if you keep forgetting things, you're not going to reach executive level.

You know why? There's no way to achieve *results* when you're forgetting!

Results come to the attention of CEOs and managers. Well, then, I want *you* to see results. That's why I'd like you to test your memory *now,* before I teach you anything.

Another thing I learned from the interviews is that *all* top executives have excellent memories, even those who seem to think they do not. Chrysler Chairman and CEO Lee Iacocca said in a *Fortune* interview, "If you care, you remember." A similar point was made during my interview with **Phyllis Barr,** Administrator for the Manhattan law firm of Pavia and Harcourt.

PB: If a client owes a million dollars — something like *that,* you remember.
HL: When a lot of money is involved — suddenly everyone's memory is terrific! Interest, motivation.
PB: People who are driven will remember.
HL: You're in an executive position — are you driven? And are you saying that most executive-level people are driven?
PB: *I'm* driven, absolutely. And in my opinion, most executives are. We're talking about ego and power. Money goes along with that. And, because they're driven, they'll remember what they have to. Because they don't want to fail, don't want to look foolish. Also, it's evident that you have the *interest* when you remember.
HL: Are you saying that if you remember well — which, in turn, shows interest — you're impressing those who may further your career? Promote you?
PB: Correct.

Saundra Malvin is Director of Administration and Executive Assistant to the Chairman at General Instrument Corporation, a Fortune 500 company. She intimated to me that she thought she had a bad memory. I told her that most people in high executive positions, even those who say they have lousy memories, have great memories. Otherwise, I don't think they'd have reached the positions they're in. I didn't believe she had a bad memory. I doubt if she'd have reached the executive level she has reached if she didn't have a better-than-average memory. "I agree; I do agree, of course," said Saundra. "Everything is relative. I just feel my memory could be better." Sure; everyone's can. That's my function.

So, I'm assuming that (a) you have a good memory and (b) you like to see results. I want to show you how *much* room for improvement there is — even for your good (or great, or lousy, or indifferent) memory. I think it's important to see almost immediate progress in order really to learn. Help me show you that progress, those *results*. Invest the few minutes needed to take the tests that follow. Each one is business-oriented; each represents a memory problem that I'm sure you face almost every business day. You don't have to take all the tests at the same sitting; rest between tests, if you like. And do them in *pencil*. You'll want to erase the answers so that you can take the tests again. Write your present score in the space provided at the left at the end of each test. The space at the right — labeled "Second time around" — is where you will put your score when you retake the test later on.

Test 1

Assume that each of the following items represents an errand you have to do or an appointment you have to keep tomorrow. Give yourself about *three* minutes to study them. Then (without looking, of course) try to write them in *correct sequence*. If one is out of sequence, all those remaining would also be incorrect. Give yourself 8 points for each one listed properly.

calculator, dress, key, book, flashlight, pin, table, cigar,

note pad, river, diamond, stapler

Score: _24 80_   Second time around: _____

Test 2

Give yourself *six* minutes to try to remember the spouses' names listed below. Then cover the top list with a piece of paper, and fill in as many blanks below as you can. Give yourself 8 points for each correct answer.

Paul Corrigan/Mary	Richard Gardner/Hortense
Albert Cohen/Estelle	Betty Yost/Bill
James Smith/Beatrice	Fred Peskowitz/Rita
Bernard Sheridan/Alice	Philip Karpel/Marilyn
Helen Sitkowski/Carl	Martin Hamilton/Delia
Gordon Fieldston/Sylvia	Lucy Battaglia/Andrew

(cover the above after six minutes)

Mr. ___Bill___ Yost   Mrs. _____ Fieldston

Mrs. _____ Peskowitz   Mrs. _____ Smith

Mrs. _____ Karpel   Mrs. _____ Corrigan

Mrs. _Estelle_ Cohen   Mrs. _____ Gardner

Mr. _____ Battaglia   Mrs. _____ Sheridan

Mrs. _____ Hamilton   Mr. _____ Sitkowski

Score: _____   *Second time around:* _____

Test 3

You want to remember some prices of items integral to your business. What you need to do is to connect the numbers to the item. Look at the price list on page 28 for about *six* minutes. Then cover it and fill in the blanks that follow. Score 12 points for each correct item.

crude oil: $18.96   gold: $460.10

pork bellies: $60.77   corn: $1.94

lease car: $541.20   coffee: $127.50

Polaroid: $42.12   computer system: $994.98

(cover the above after six minutes)

corn: _____   Polaroid: _____

lease car: _____   coffee: _____

gold: _____   crude oil: _____

computer system: _____   pork bellies: _____

Score: __60__   *Second time around:* _____

Test 4

Look at the following list of "hidden objects" for about *four* minutes.
Each item listed is followed by its hiding place — the pen is hidden
under the plate, and so on. Try to remember what's hidden where.
Then cover the list and try to fill in the blanks that follow. If the item
is listed, fill in the hiding place; if the hiding place is listed, fill in the
item that's hidden there. Score 10 points for each correct answer.

pen/plate   credit card/desk blotter

nail file/drinking glass   gold cuff links/steel file cabinet

stamp/matchbook cover   extra eyeglasses/behind picture frame birth certificate/vault

bracelet/tucked in glove

address book/under bed

lipstick/shirt drawer

(cover the above after four minutes)

credit card: _____DEsK BloTTer_____ ✓ cuff links: _____STeeL_____ ✓

matchbook cover: _____STock_____ ✓ address book: _____UNder B_____ ✓

vault: _____BiRTH CirtTe_____ ✓ nail file: _____GLoss_____ ✓

shirt drawer: _____LipsTicK_____ ✓ pen: _____PLoTe_____ ✓

glove: _____BroceleT_____ ✓ eyeglasses: _____PicTure_____ ✓

Score: _____100_____ *Second time around:* _____

Test 5

Here are ten of the items from Test 1. They're in a different order and they're *numbered*. They may represent the ten points you want to make during a sales presentation. Try to memorize both number and item. Give yourself about *seven* minutes. Then cover them, and fill in the blanks on the next page. Score 10 points for each correct answer.

7. diamond

2. river

5. book

9. key

10. pin

1. note pad

4. table

6. cigar

8. flashlight

3. dress

(cover the above after seven minutes)

1: _PRO_   6: _AFR. Crlws_

2: _R\wvR_   7: _Dimnd_

3: _DRugs_   8: _FlsDLits_

4: _Table_   9: _____   K

5: _Book_   10: _Piw_

Score: _40_   Second time around: _80_

Test 6

Give yourself *six* minutes; try to connect each person's name (only the surname is fine) and position to the corporate name. (These are all real people, positions, and companies.) Then cover the information and fill in as many of the blanks as you can. Score 10 points for each correct one.

Al Clausi, Vice President, General Foods Corporation

George Konogeris, Vice President, Kinney Shoe Corporation

Ralph Destino, Chairman, Cartier, Inc.

Philip Bossert, Director of Sales, *Business Week*

Scott Marcus, President, Evan-Picone Shoes

Harvey Leeds, Vice President of Promotion, Epic Records

Ellen Hassman, President, AC and R Direct, Inc.

Frank AtLee, Vice President, American Cyanamid Corporation

Bernadette Skubly-Butts, Account Executive, Air France

William Seco, Vice President of Sales, EDP World, Inc.

(cover the above after six minutes)

Mr. AtLee: _____   Ms. Skubly-Butts: _____

Mr. Marcus: _____   Mr. Leeds: _____

Mr. Seco: _____   Mr. Clausi: _____

Ms. Hassman: _____   Mr. Bossert: _____

Mr. Konogeris: _____   Mr. Destino: _____

Score: _____   *Second time around:* _____

Test 7

If you solve these out-of-thinking-rut tests within the given time slots, give yourself a hug. You won't be taking them again — but you will be making business friends take 'em, I'll wager. The solutions are elsewhere in the book. You'll find them as you read, study, learn.

a. Can you add only one symbol to the following Roman numeral and thus change it to an even number between 5 and 10?

IX

You should solve this within *four* minutes.

b. Make the following line *shorter* without erasing, without cutting or tearing, without using opaquing fluid or tape, and without folding the page, covering it, or reproducing it in any way. Think about it for no more than *six* minutes.

_____

c. Shown below is the one martini you had during your business luncheon. Use four matches to lay out the martini glass. The head of a fifth match can be the olive or Gibson onion. Challenge: Move only *two* matches to bring the olive *outside* the glass. Do *not* touch the "olive." The glass must end up shaped exactly as shown. (Hint: It need not necessarily face in the same direction.) You've got *five* minutes.

Test 8

Here's a sixteen-digit number. You've got about *two and a half minutes* to memorize it. Cover it, then write it; try to get all the digits in the correct sequence. Score 6 points for each digit you place correctly.

7 5 1 4 3 2 6 8 0 3 5 9 2 1 1 3

Score: _30_   Second time around: _____

75 143 068 2 92 1 3

Test 9

You enter a room in which you will momentarily be giving a presentation of your new advertising campaign. You're introduced to twelve new people, important people. Here they are. Take about *eight* minutes to meet them all. Try to remember who's who, of course. I'll have them walk by you at the end of this chapter — in a different order and without their name tags — so you can try to fill in the correct name for each. Give yourself 8 points for each person you remember.

MR. WEBB

MR. WOODBURY

MS. SPEERS

DR. KAISER

MS. BEACON

MR. WITHERSPOON

MR. CAMPBELL

MS. PATTERSON

MR. ASHBERG

MR. PIERCE

MS. PETROVSKI

MR. EISENBERG

When you reach the end of this chapter — not now — fill in the blanks where these people are shown again. Then come back to this test, check your answers, and fill in your score.

Score: _no_   *Second time around:* _____

Test 10

You're an executive for a department store. Different items have different style codes — just letters, or letters and numbers. You'd like to remember them. Try with these ten. Take about *four* minutes. Then cover this information and fill in the test blanks. Give yourself 10 points for each correct answer.

men's suits: HT   computers: RN1

diamond rings: BC86   bill clips: L2R

cordless telephones: DF   pottery: EM4

lingerie: WR   furniture: SL8

wallets: GW   luggage: 7LR

(cover the above after four minutes)

furniture: _____   wallets: _____

luggage: _____L W_____   cordless telephones: __L__

pottery: _____   computers: _____

men's suits: ___H T___   lingerie: ___W T___

bill clips: _____   diamond rings: ___BC 86___

Score: _18_   *Second time around:* _____

Test 11

Take about *nine* minutes to try to memorize these telephone numbers and to whom they belong. Then cover them and fill in the ensuing blanks as best you can. Give yourself 10 points for each *entirely* correct number. (One digit wrong or out of sequence and you'd be dialing a wrong number.)

garage: 243-6340   watch repair: 557-0947

stationery: 914-5631   doctor: 292-1821

library: 641-4414   bank: 324-7892

Mr. Forrest: 474-2936   meeting planner: 741-1248

tailor: 389-9484   restaurant: 534-9625

(*cover the above after nine minutes*)

meeting planner: _____   library: _____

Mr. Forrest: _____   restaurant: _____

doctor: _____   tailor: _____

watch repair: _____   bank: _____

garage: _____   stationery: _____

Score: _____   *Second time around:* _____

Test 12

These are legitimate area codes. There are eleven of them, because one may be yours! No fair; that one shouldn't be considered or scored. So, try to memorize as many as you can in about *four* minutes. Then, cover them and fill in as many blanks as you can. The areas will be listed in a different order. Score 10 points for each one you remember correctly.

West Virginia: 304

Manhattan, N.Y.: 212

Toronto, Canada: 416

San Diego, Calif.: 619

Milwaukee, Wis.: 414

Pittsburgh, Pa.: 412

Topeka, Kans.: 913

Nashville, Tenn.: 615

Los Angeles, Calif.: 213

Wyoming: 307

Spokane, Wash.: 509

(cover the above after four minutes)

Nashville: _____

Pittsburgh: _____

Topeka: _____

Los Angeles: _____213_____

West Virginia: ____304_____

Toronto: _____416_____

Manhattan: _____

Spokane: _____

San Diego: _____

Milwaukee: _____414_____

Wyoming: _____

Score: _____

Second time around: _____

Don't be discouraged by your bad scores; don't get too excited over your pretty good scores. When you take the tests again (when I tell you to), no matter *what* your scores were this first time, you'll amaze yourself. You *really* will.

Coffee break is over. The twelve new people you were introduced to earlier walk by you as they reenter the room. You would really like to put the right name to the right face. Turn the page and give it a try.

Ashbury

Campbell

Petrovski

Woodberry

Speer

An article about **Alan Greenberg,** Chairman and CEO of Bear Stearns Company, appeared in *Forbes,* on September 7, 1987. Headline: "To many on Wall St., Alan Greenberg is one of the shrewdest players around." The feature story in the August 31, 1987, issue of *U.S. News & World Report* mentioned that Alan earned $5.7 million in salary in 1986. Headline: "Alan Greenberg can't help it if he's making too much money!" Alan said to me:

> Someone with a good memory absolutely just plain stands out. Yes, it would come to the attention of the people at the top, including me, because a good memory is *so* important in this business. My salespeople *must* remember investors' names, how to reach them quickly if they need a fast buy or sell okay. They have to be able to remember changing prices of certain stocks, which client owns those stocks, stock symbols, computer codes, appointments.
>
> The essential thing when starting out in any job is to get recognized, noticed, by your superiors. If you have a terrific memory, if you remember something that somebody else forgot, supervisors and managers pick up on that very quickly — at least if they're intelligent, and most superiors and managers are.

5

The Biggest Little Nuisance in Business: Absentmindedness

Save Precious Minutes Searching —
A Simple Trick Ends Absentmindedness

"I Just Had It in My Hand!"

I started my career as an entertainer, performing feats of memory. I wrote the whole act in ten minutes. It was simple: I just listed the major memory problems. Then I devised a demonstration to show that each of those problems *could* be solved. The number-one memory problem that came to mind was "names and faces." I thought, "I'll remember the names and faces of all the people in my audience to demonstrate that it need not be a problem." I did — and still do whenever I do a personal appearance.

The next problem I thought of was that of hiding valuables in a "safe place" and then forgetting *which* safe place. I devised a demonstration called "objects and hiding places." People would call out an object, a silly (or difficult) hiding place, and a number. The

41

information was written in that numbered space on a blackboard. Then someone would call out a number, an object, or a hiding place and I'd instantly supply the other two items. "What's hidden in the mattress?" "The Ping-Pong ball, and it's in number fifteen!" People would test me at any time throughout my performance.

Now what in the world does remembering/knowing where you hid a favorite pair of cuff links or earrings have to do with raising the level of your productivity in business? With helping to give you that business edge? With making you a better executive, manager, foreman, employee? It has quite a bit to do with it. (First, of course, there are times when you can't separate your personal life from your business life.)

In the July 1987 issue of *Self* magazine, an article appeared purporting to show how to find hidden items. It was based on research done by Eugene Winograd, Ph.D, and Robert M. Soloway. The research suggested that people hide things in strange and unlikely places because they think it's easier to remember such places. This is because they've heard — perhaps from *me!* — that "unusual events are remembered better than ordinary events." I've said it (written it, screamed it, engraved it) for over three decades: It's the mundane, everyday things that we tend to forget. The unusual, the violent, the obscene, the extraordinary, the bizarre, the ridiculous are easily remembered.

But now these researchers tell us that it isn't so. They talk about the "generation-recognition strategy." What that means is that you generate (mentally) the places the vital item can possibly be, hoping that when (and if) you hit the correct one you'll know it. But, they say, if it's an unusual place, you may never hit on it.

So they decided that no matter how "unforgettable unusual locations seem, they are harder to remember than common ones." They give reasons for this, the first one being that "there's no association trigger." (They're absolutely right!) If you hide an extra key in an antique vase, when you need the key, you think, "Where's the key?" not "What's in the antique vase?" (Absolutely right!) They go on to say that unless someone happens to say "antique vase," you'll never think of where you hid the key. (Absolutely *wrong!*)

I could have told them that the simple concept upon which *all* memory is based — the reminder principle — can be brought into play. You don't have to wait until someone "happens to say 'antique vase' " — no, you simply have to *force* "key" to *remind* you of "antique vase" whenever you ask yourself, or think, "Where's the key?"

The principle of *original awareness* is automatically applied at the same time. We're talking about an absentmindedness problem here. And the way to solve absentmindedness in *any* area is to be originally aware of the usually unconscious action. I'll get into that more specifically later. Right now, the point is that you *can* remember unusual things and locations better, once you *know how* to use the *reminder* and *original-awareness* ideas. The way I remembered made-up — hypothetical — objects and hiding places during my act is exactly the way you can remember where you've hidden an actual item that's important to you.

Of course you need an "association trigger." All that really means is that you need a *reminder*. Follow this simple rule: **Make one thing remind you of the other.** How? *At the moment* of the action, form a silly picture (association) in your mind connecting the two vital pieces of information — the object and the hiding place. Make it a silly, ridiculous, or *impossible* picture. *As* you place the extra key into the vase, *visualize* yourself sticking that expensive vase into a keyhole (shattering the vase) and opening the door! (You're using the vase *instead of* the key.) *Really see* that picture in your mind's eye and you will have accomplished a great deal. You've used a bit of imagination, and you've focused your attention, which means you've *paid* attention; you've pinpointed your concentration at that moment onto the problem of the moment: you've forced yourself to be *originally aware* of where you're hiding the key. It's the ridiculousness, the impossibility, of the picture that takes the information out of the mundane, that makes it *work*.

And it took a split second. Now, days later or a month later, you ask yourself, "Where did I hide that extra key?" If you originally formed a silly, impossible picture in your mind connecting key and antique vase, just thinking of *key* will automatically make you think of *vase;* one must *remind* you of the other. The "generation-recognition strategy" no longer applies — it becomes pure psychobabble. There's obviously no earthly reason to "generate" different possible places. None at all. Thinking of the important item itself *tells* you where you hid it!

You hide an expensive pen in your lingerie drawer. Visualize the ink squirting out of that pen, all over your fine lingerie, ruining it all. I assure you, you'll always know where that pen is; all you have to do is *think* "pen"! You want to put two special concert tickets in a safe place. How about under the typewriter? Good idea. Same problem. How will you remember? At the moment you place those tickets *form an association*. See (visualize, imagine) two large tickets *typing*. Or see a typewriter (all dressed up) entering Carnegie Hall, or wherever. Or see a gigantic typewriter *performing* the concert, playing the piano. I'm offering more than one choice for silly pictures, as I'll continue to do. All you really need is one picture, and you're better off thinking of it yourself. I mean that you should try to conjure up your *own* silly pictures for any similar situation, even one that exactly matches one of my examples. That's the point: you're *forced* to *think* about it.

Three more important points:

1. Be sure the picture you select involves only the two vital items whenever possible. It is *not* necessary (or wise) to make up an "action story." You do want *action* — but just between the two vital items, in one quick (but vivid) picture.
2. Although "thinking" the picture will probably do it for you, it's best to make the slight extra effort actually to *see* the picture you select. The odds are that thinking it will be the same as seeing it in your mind's eye. That's so for most people. But until you're sure, make that minimal effort to *see the picture*. The truth is, that little bit of effort is what makes the technique work! It forces you to pinpoint your concentration as you never have before.
3. Form the association *at the moment* you hide the item. If you wait to do it later, you may have forgotten where you hid the thing when later rolls around.

Right now, at this moment, even if you didn't consciously make the associations (just reading them was probably sufficient), don't you know where the key is hidden? The concert tickets? How do you think I memorized the objects and hiding places during my performance years ago? Exactly as I've just explained. How could I possibly forget that the Ping-Pong ball was hidden under the mattress when I "saw" two mattresses playing Ping-Pong? (I also remembered a number; it's easy. I put one other item into my picture, an item that represented or *meant* a number to me. That is explained elsewhere in this book.)

And if you don't believe, yet, that this technique works, works *perfectly,* go back to chapter 4 and retake the test in which this technique should be used — Test 4. I want you to *see your progress.*

Peter Kougasian *(Assistant District Attorney, Director of Legal Staff Training, Manhattan, New York):* Absentmindedness is aggravating and it's time-consuming. The reason it's so aggravating is *because* it's so time-consuming — at the office, but also at home.

Quite a few of the executives I interviewed told me that often they came late to an early morning business appointment because of time spent searching for a personal item (a wallet, keys, eyeglasses, concert or airline tickets, and so on) that they'd either "just had in their hand" or had hidden "in a safe place." So even what you do on *your* time can affect you *business-wise,* efficiency-wise. And of course these memory techniques work the same at home, at the office — anywhere.

When I asked whether absentmindedness was also directly a problem in the office, in business, most all my interviewees replied that indeed it was.

Phyllis Barr: Absolutely; time is money. I don't want to take the time to search for glasses — or anything else.

Ruth Mass: Yes, it's definitely a problem. Always looking for my glasses, pen, purse. It's the interruptions that usually do it. Oh, yes — teach us to remember where a thing is put when we're interrupted. Every minute lost, costs.

J. K. Hartman, Managing Director and CEO of Scudder, Stevens and Clark, the investment-counseling firm, feels the same way — that absentmindedness is aggravating and time-consuming. He does, how-ever, have his own little tricks. And these tricks eliminate certain additional kinds of absentmindedness.

My policy is if I'm thinking of something, do it *then*. If I'm shaving and I think, "I should have written down so-and-so to remember it," I'll stop shaving and write it down *then*. People think I'm crazy sometimes, stopping what I'm doing to do this thing I don't want to forget. I may be crazy — but I don't forget! So, one of my tricks is do it then and there.

I use another little trick. When I do a mundane little thing, I say out loud, to myself, what I've just done, or what I'm doing. And that'll help me remember, a week later, that I did it. If, when I use my deodorant in the morning, I say out loud, "I am using my deodorant," then I don't have to wonder later, "Did I use my deodorant this morning?" I *know* I did.

The same idea would work for things like "I am turning on my telephone answering machine"; "I am unplugging the coffeepot"; "I am locking my door." Jerry Hartman says, "I'm just too busy to take the time to worry about whether or not I used my deodorant, unplugged the coffeepot, or other mundane little things. I manage a corporation that invests millions of dollars for clients. My mind has to be on *that*."

Jerry is on the right track. Although these problems are not exactly the same as remembering where you hid a valued item, they are related. And he is following one of my rules for eliminating absent-mindedness: **Make sure your mind is present, not absent, at the specific moment during which a mundane action is taking place.**

Saying to yourself, out loud, just before putting down a business report to answer the phone, "I've stopped reading the report on page twelve," will most likely eliminate dog-eared pages. You'll know that you have to open to page 12 when you want to continue reading that report. Saying (out loud), "I've just turned on my answering machine," is *forcing* your mind to think of that action at that instant. At that instant, you're eliminating absentmindedness via the simple expedient of forcing yourself to be *present*minded!

Saundra Malvin: Absentmindedness is bothersome and time-consuming, and time is money.

One bank manager (who prefers to remain anonymous) exaggerated a bit, I'm sure, when he complained:

Harry, I must be getting old. I waste three months out of every year, lately, searching my desk, my files, my office, my secretary's desk, for something I just had in my hands. Often it's an inconsequential thing like my pencil or a rubber band, or it can be an important piece of paper. You say you can teach me to save that time? You'd also save my life!

I doubt that he wastes three months of every year — but I'll go along with a few weeks. "Getting old" doesn't have much to do with it, since young executives complain of the same problem. Recently, a Harvard Business School study revealed that the average executive (no matter what his or her age) wastes about thirty minutes a day searching for things on his or her desk. Add a bit of time wasted searching through locations other than desks and, yes, that totals a few wasted weeks.

Well, the way to save that time — the solution — can be to *shout* where you're temporarily placing something, just to force yourself to *think* about what you're doing at that particular instant, to force your mind to be *present*. But I don't know how many offices would continue to function normally if a number of my students were there shouting to themselves!

No, there's an easier way to eliminate *any* sort of absentmindedness — a *silent* way. And that way again is to form an association, to *see* a silly picture in your mind's eye, which is *the same as forcing attention*.

Michael K. Stanton: In a law firm, in *this* law firm, a strong memory is crucial.

HL: You just took a long phone call about a case and I heard you use names of people and places. You referred to dates and events without looking at a file. Can you do that with other cases?

MKS: When I have deadlines and cutoffs and particular items in particular cases, I know them.

HL: How many cases do you handle at one time? For example, right now?

MKS: Forty-five.

HL: You're personally involved in forty-five cases?

MKS: Directly responsible for, not just personally involved.

HL: Does that mean that right now if someone came in and asked you a question about any one of those forty-five cases, you'd have an answer?

MKS: I'd better. I'll tell you what that takes, and what I needed as I worked my way up to my present position — what I need now, and what every person at executive level, or working toward executive level, needs. And that is to know how to apply effective attention.

Here's how to apply *effective attention* the silent way. Let's say you're holding Mr. Forrest's file in your hands. You're interrupted and your attention is diverted. You reach to your attaché case and slip the file inside — a mundane, habitual action that you don't *think* about at all. When the problem that interrupted you is attended to, you might look for the Forrest file immediately or a bit later. Since your mind was absent when you automatically slipped the file into your attaché case, you have no idea where it is. Therefore the cry, ''I just had it in my hand!'' (You can't say, ''I forgot where I put it,'' because you never *remembered* in the first place!)

Solution? Make sure you do remember in the first place — that you *are* originally aware. Take one split second at the instant of the ordinarily automatic action to form the association; see a mind picture that will work as an *automatic reminder*. For example, *as* you slip the Forrest file into the case, *see a forest* growing in your attaché case. Or hundreds of attaché cases growing like trees, in a forest. Be sure to *really see* the picture you select. It takes no more than a split second; no need to break mental or physical stride. But you have forced yourself to **think of the action at the moment of the action** — you've made yourself originally aware of it. That's the rule. And that's effective attention.

I guarantee that when you next think of the Forrest file, you'll think forest, forest growing in your attaché case! You'll simply reach into the case. You will hardly be aware that you've applied a system that made you "presentminded," that eliminates absentmindedness.

If you drop the file into your outgoing mail bin, you might visualize a forest growing out of that bin. If you drop it onto your office coffee table, see a forest growing on that table, or see tables, instead of trees, growing in a forest. If you see that picture in your mind, you've forced a second's worth of effective attention, and that's all that's necessary.

Joseph V. Casale (*President, Active Concern, Inc., representing Phoenix Insurance Companies):* Oh, that "I just had it in my hand" thing. I do wish I could eliminate that problem.

Are you always searching for your eyeglasses? Form a simple habit — and that's all it is, habit — by forming associations three or five times. Simply connect eyeglasses to *where you're putting them* via a silly picture. Example: You're rushing out and leave your glasses on the table next to a potted plant. Keep on rushing, but *as* you put them down, visualize a pair of eyeglasses watering your potted plant! Or see yourself wearing a potted plant over each eye *instead of* eyeglasses. You've paid effective attention for a split second to that split-second action — which means you *thought about it* for that little slice of time. You never stopped, no time has been wasted. And no time *will* be wasted when you need your eyeglasses. The instant you want them, you will have a built-in reminder. Think "eyeglasses" and you'll "see" them watering a potted plant. You'll just *know* that they're there, near the plant.

Sticking your pencil into your hair takes no time at all. Trying to remember where it is, could. The solution is the same. *Think about it* at the moment you put it there. But don't you see? *That's* the problem. It's difficult to think of a fleeting, automatic action. That's why you need a technique that *forces* that instant's thought, which amounts to paying effective attention. I've taught you the technique. *As* you push the pencil into your hair visualize it (*feel* it) going into your head, point first! Now you couldn't forget where that pencil is if you tried!

It boils down to *original awareness*. "Our thoughts are so fleeting," wrote Henry Hazlitt, "no device for trapping them should be overlooked." Don't overlook the device I've just taught you for trapping those fleeting thoughts!

That same device is used for the mundane "little aggravators" — the "Did I turn on the answering machine?," "Did I lock the office door?" kind of thing. Grab your mind by the scruff of the neck, force it to pay attention, by forming a silly association. See yourself turning on your answering machine with your *ear*. See yourself putting your head or your foot or your eyeball into the keyhole when you lock your door. That's all. It's the same as, but more effective and quieter than, shouting it out loud. You've forced yourself to *think* about the mundane action, to be *originally aware* of it; you've forced your mind to be *present* for that split second — and that's all it takes.

Do you want to be *sure* to take, say, your passport when you leave your office? Associate it with the last thing you *pay attention to* or notice when you leave. *Make* this last thing remind you of your passport. If it's the elevator, visualize the doors of that elevator opening and a million passports falling or flying out. Or see the elevator *being* a gigantic passport. *That* will remind you to run back and get your passport, or to check if you did take it. If it's *very* important, use a backup: associate passport with one other last thing — for example, your taxi. Visualize a gigantic passport driving it. You'll still have time to go back for the passport. This technique will help you remember anything — an umbrella, a book, theater tickets — you need to take from office or home.

Do you get great ideas in the middle of the night? Are they usually gone in the morning? Is it too much trouble to turn on the light and jot something down or to scribble indecipherable notes in the dark? Tell you what — the next time you're hit with that creative thought in the middle of the night, reach over and turn your clock face-down, or dump your cigarettes on the floor, or toss a slipper to the other side of the room! Do *anything* that will grab your attention in the morning. *That's* your reminder.

Are you thinking that this will remind you that you had a thought but not *what* that thought was? Make the out-of-place thing *tell* you. If the thought has to do with computers, as you toss your slipper, associate slipper to computer with a silly picture (a computer wearing slippers, perhaps), and go back to sleep. You'll remember not only that you had a thought but what that thought was about.

All these techniques require immediate action, sometimes physical (tossing your slipper) and always mental (forming the association). That's not a unique idea. Just about every executive I interviewed uses the "briefcase trick" to remember to take certain papers from office to home (or vice versa). That trick is to put the papers (or whatever) into your briefcase beforehand. They all said something like, "My briefcase is an extension of my arm, so I *never* forget that." And they all agreed that the papers must be placed into the case the *instant* you think of them. *That* is the key. If it isn't done at that moment, you'll forget. **Don't let that fleeting thought escape.**

What do you do if you're on your way to the office and you think of something that should be put into your case immediately? You can't do it if the item is in your office and you're not there. Perhaps it's a letter from John Zimmerman. Visualize a man simmering (boiling — *simmer man*) on your desk, on your secretary, in your office coat closet — any place that you'll *notice* when you arrive. That will remind you to put that letter into your case immediately.

This technique for applying effective attention enables you to be *present*minded, which, of course, *must* eliminate absentmindedness. The visualization concept, the silly mental pictures, are basic tools for remembering — and they will be applied in slightly different ways, throughout this book.

Fredrica S. Friedman *(Vice President, Associate Publisher, and Executive Editor, Little, Brown and Company):* There's no doubt that you need a very good memory to be a good editor. After all, an editor must hold an entire book in her head. She must remember the author's theme and subplots to know if he sustains them throughout the story — and this is as true for nonfiction as for fiction. And an editor must remember that a character has black hair on page 31 in order to know that something is askew if the same character is a blond on page 108; a male character can't be a great lover on page 14 and totally inadequate (at least not without an explanation) on page 96. Since continuity of the entire book is essential, an editor needs an excellent memory.

And while manufacturers may deal with widgets, an editor deals daily, hourly, with people — authors, agents, her publishing colleagues. In fact, her success in this personal-service business is directly related to these human relationships. It is important, then, that she remember her author's former books, and their references to future books. It is crucial in personal relationships to keep in mind the details of authors' and agents' lives. I'd better not say to you, Harry, "How's your wife, Alice?" when your wife's name is Renée. And when you call me to inquire about your first printing and your advertising schedule, I need to recall *all* the distinguishing attributes and plans for *your* book. When you add to this that I may be involved with several dozen books at one time, and as many authors and agents, I could not maintain my level of productivity without a highly trained memory.

6

The *Trick* That Makes Numbers Easy to Remember

For Prices, Stock Quotations, Sales Reports, Style Numbers, and More

We live in a number-oriented society; probably the most important things we have to remember in business are numbers. How could the business wheels continue to turn without *somebody* remembering vital information such as prices, style numbers, stock quotes, and so forth? Yet, where memory is concerned, numbers are like quicksilver — the more you try to grasp them, the farther away they spurt! For most, numbers are the most difficult things to remember because they are abstract and therefore cannot be visualized. A number is a concept: 5 is one less than 6 and one higher than 4. Well, I'll start to show you in this chapter that numbers *can* be visualized. To begin with, let me assure you that . . .

We, human beings, do not — repeat, do *not* — forget. What we do is we *don't remember in the first place*. Therein lies both the problem and the *solution* to the memory enigma: Remember in the first place, be *originally aware,* and there simply *is* no forgetting! "Sure, easier said than done," you're mumbling. "Just how in the world do I do that? With me things usually go into one ear and right out the other." Yes, usually, but not always, right? If Chicken Little ran up to you and shouted, "Come with me — I want to show you where the sky is falling down," there'd be a *stop* somewhere between your ears, and you'd remember it. And if you did see the sky falling down, you'd certainly remember that — forever!

Well, okay. *Of course* you'd remember a chicken telling you that the sky is falling. You'd be *originally aware* of that unless you were dead. Problem: Most if not all of the information you need to remember doesn't fall into that category. Certainly business data is not usually part of the Chicken Little sky-is-falling category. Aha! But you see all, *any* information and business data can be *placed* into that category by making it interesting, different, unique. And the first step in that direction is to make meaningless things meaningful. It's obviously easier to remember something that makes sense, that is meaningful, than something that's not.

A client mentioned to me that he just couldn't remember the letters of the alphabet his firm uses as part of its style number system. HN stands for men's shirts, DR means ladies' slacks, and so forth. I wrote the following on a piece of paper:

Z A Y B X C W D V E U F T G S H R I Q J P K O L N M

He said that he saw no rhyme or reason there. I explained:

Well, what I did was to write the alphabet, as quickly as I could, forward and backward *at the same time!* Follow along. Start with the second-from-left letter, A, and move to every other letter. You see? It goes to M, in proper sequence. Now move to the left the same way — starting with N and following every other letter. You'll go from N to Z in proper sequence. Problem is, I've *yet* to find a practical use for it!

It'll seem weird, but here's how I memorized this particular sequence. I made up and *visualized* a silly story a long time ago: I was talking to a bee and a few eggs; I said, "Say, bee [ZAYB], eggs, see water? [XCW] The view? [DVEU]" As I indicated the view, someone gashed my foot — a **foot gasher** [FTGSHR]. I told him that he had the IQ of a jeep [IQJP] and that I'd call him a bad name — *call name* [KOLNM]! Look at the sequence now:

Say bee	eggs see water	the view
ZAYB	XCW	DVEU

foot gasher	IQ jeep	call name
FTGSHR	IQJP	KOLNM

Seems silly, I know, but visualize those sillinesses in order. Give it a few minutes, and you'll know the alphabet forward and backward.

There are better ways to remember specific letters of the alphabet, based on "sound-alikes." The basic idea, though, is to make meaningless things meaningful. That's one of the greatests aids to memory. But we often *do* form acronyms to serve as memory aids. That's okay, up to a point.

HL: So you consider the facts you remember your professional body of knowledge?
Philip A. Bossert: Yes, everything is. And mentioning an acronym reminds me. There's a formula in this business — AIDA. Attention, Interest, Decision, Action. Advertising has to get attention, grasp interest, force a decision (that's why ad offers usually end on a specific date) and then action — make the reader *buy*.

Years ago (I don't know if it's valid now) home insurance brokers would sell "extended coverage." When asked what that covered, they were able to answer promptly because they remembered the fictional name W. C. Shaver: **w**ind, **c**ommotion, **s**moke, **h**ail, **a**ircraft, **v**ehicle, **e**xplosion, **r**iot. (**Joseph V. Casale** told me that he, and many other insurance brokers, remembered a strong selling point by thinking of a *meaningless* group of letters: WWYDIYIST — What would you do if your income stopped tomorrow? Good selling point; it just seems to me that trying to remember a meaningless group of letters is not much of a memory *aid*.)

A technique similar in concept but more effective in its application can be used to remember numbers. As a matter of fact, the acronym AIDA describes my systems: they force attention, force interest, make you decide to remember, then show you how to associate (as you'll see). Okay; you know that certain retail businesses mark their items with a letter code to tell the employees of the firm the price without the customer's knowing. It's a simple coding device. All that's needed is a word or phrase consisting of ten letters, with no letters repeated. *Ten* letters because you want each letter to represent a different one of the ten possible single digits. A nine-letter word or phrase is just as good; an X is used as the tenth letter. Any word or phrase will do, so long as all the vital people remember it (and know how to spell). Check these:

1	2	3	4	5	6	7	8	9	0
M	I	C	R	O	W	A	V	E	S
B	L	A	C	K	S	M	I	T	H
P	I	C	K	L	E	D	H	A	M
M	A	R	Y	C.	J	O	N	E	S
N	A	K	E	D	G	I	R	L	S
C	O	S	T	P	R	I	C	E	X

Assume that "microwaves" is the code word; then WCC would represent the price $633. Or, $6.33, according to the business, the item. It's a matter of simple substitution: MAS — M is the first letter (1), A is the seventh letter (7), and S is the last letter (0). What else can MAS mean *but* $1.70 or $170?

VRM is, could only be, 841. Now, that's not a bad way to remember that three-digit number. For a five-digit number you would have, for example, EOVIA (95827). And so on. Not bad. Not very good either. Why would it be easier to remember VRM than 841? What makes EOVIA more meaningful than 95827? *Both* are really meaningless. The *idea,* however, has merit. Letters can be used to *represent* numbers.

One of the old (also not very good) systems for remembering numbers, using letters, is to use words containing the equivalent *number* of letters to *represent* the individual digits. You'd have to come up with a phrase or sentence consisting of words with the right number of letters that somehow related to what you wanted to recall. For example:

WITH   PICTURE   TUBE

(4 letters)   (7 letters)   (4 letters)

might help you remember that a television set retails for $474. To remember pi to five places (3.1415), you might use:

MAY   I   HAVE   A   **PIECE?**

(3)   (1)   (4)   (1)   (5)

It's an interesting but not very practical approach. What would you come up with for, say, 7471075042732 — no matter what it represented? There's *got* to be a better way. And there is. A *great* way! A fascinating and fun way to use letters to enable you to remember numbers. And I mean to remember numbers as no one ever could before — practically to *read* them off your mind as if reading them from a computer screen.

It's *so* easy. Just make each of the alphabet's main *consonant sounds* represent one of the ten numerical digits from 1 to 0. Let the sound that the letter **T** makes always represent or *mean* the digit 1. The letter **D** makes basically the same sound, so that, too, means 1. Let the **n** sound represent the digit 2, the **m** sound the digit 3.

I'll teach you to remember all the letters of the alphabet easily — in any combination, that is — later. Right now, remembering these specific letter sounds and their numerical equivalents is child's play, literally. Play this game: Think of the letter **T** made up of digit 1's. One 1 is perpendicular, the other (the crossbar) is lying on the first one.

Or, if you like, think of the typewritten letter **T** as having *one* downstroke.

A typewritten **n** has *two* downstrokes — so the sound of **n** means 2. A typewritten **m** has *three* downstrokes; count 'em. Or, turn an **m** on its side and it looks exactly like a 3. Or, think of one of our large firms — the *3M* Corporation. These little reminders work even for children because they're so easy and obvious.

R is 4. Just think of the last sound in the word fou**R**. Or look at a printed **R**; with only a small stretch of the imagination it looks like a stick figure of a golfer about to tee off — and he yells, "Fore!" Think of that for a second or two.

L is 5. The Roman numeral for **50** is **L**. Or hold up your open left hand, thumb extended to the right, as if signaling "stop." Those *5* fingers form the shape of an **L**. Or, visualize an *el* (elevated) train with *5* cars.

J is 6. The digit 6 is *almost* the mirror image of a **J**:

$$6\ \text{J}$$

Silly? Yes. But think about it for a second or two, and you've set a reminder. A soft **g** (as in "general") makes the same sound, so that, too, represents 6, because, it's the sounds that are important here. **Ch** and **sh** also mean 6, since they're virtually the same sounds. When making all of these sounds, the tip of the tongue curls downward and touches the inner side of your lower teeth.

The sound made by the letter **K** will always represent 7. Want a memory aid for that — which you'll need only at first to register the information? You could visualize a **7**-layer **cake**. I like this better: a right-side-up and an almost-upside-down 7 will form a **K**. Look:

K or hard **c** (as in "crazy") or hard **g** (as in "go") mean 7.

And, a handwritten small **f** has two loops, one above the other, just as does the digit 8:

Put a "tail" at the center of that 8 and it looks like a handwritten **f**. If you prefer, think "I *ate* (8) **f**ood." So, the sound **f** — or **v** or **ph** (same sound) — represents 8. The digit 9 is easy; look at it in a mirror and you'll see a **P**. So the sound **P** — or **B** (same pursed lips, or blowing sound) — means 9.

The last one, 0 (zero or cipher), is represented by the **s**, **z**, soft **c** (as in "cent") sound. Your reminder is that **z**ero and **c**ipher both start with the hissing sound. That's all there is. If you paid attention to the reminders, you should already have them memorized, and that's the same as *knowing* them.

Go over these once or twice, going by the sounds not the letters. Use the sounds because individual letters can make different sounds in English, like the hard or soft **c**, or the different **t** sounds in "hot" (meaning 1) and "caution" (meaning 6). Once you know this Phonetic Number/Alphabet, you'll always know it, since you'll be using it all the time.

1 = T, D	6 = J, sh, ch, soft g
2 = n	7 = K, hard c, hard g
3 = m	8 = f, v, ph
4 = R	9 = P, B
5 = L	0 = z, s, soft c

If you had trouble with any of them, even slight hesitation, just go over the reminders, the memory aids, I gave you. And you'll know them. You'll also know them out of order and inside out. That means that you should be able to fill in the blanks at the top of the next page, quickly. Try it.

4 = R	n = 2	sh =	1 = T or D
0 = Z	P,B =	7 = K	v =
6 = 3	L = 5	5 = L	T = 1
3 = M	8 = f	9 = P	2 = N
R = 4	s =	soft g =	D =
hard g =	ch =	m = 3	hard c =

That's all there is to the Phonetic Number/Alphabet. Plus these few points: The vowels, **aeiou**, are "wild cards," the connectors. They have no numerical value; they just make it easy to form words and phrases, as you'll see. For example, **belt** is 951. The "soft" consonants **w**, **h**, and **y** (*why*) have no value either (although the **h**, of course, changes the sound of some letters, as when it follows a **c**). The **th** sound is considered the same as **t**: it represents 1.

Double letters represent only one digit because they make *one* sound. "**Butter**" is 914; "**pillow**" is 95. The word "**attention**" breaks down, or transposes, to 1262 (**tt** is 1, **n** is 2, **t** [**sh** sound] is 6, **n** is 2). Silent letters have no value, because they have no sound. So, "**climb**" is 753, *not* 7539; the **b** is silent. "**Knot**" is 21 and "**bomb**" is 93. Got it? If you do, you've learned one of the most important things ever when it comes to remembering numbers. You simply can't imagine how helpful it will be. Stay with me.

Here's a short quiz, just to make sure you've "got" it. Transpose the following to the proper digits:

printer = _____   aggravate = _____

desk = _____   clearing = _____

collar = _____   ashen = _____

tenement = _____   placed = _____

crayon = _____   special = _____

elbow = _____   gigantic = _____

Lorayne = _____   silliness = _____

You can check whether or not your answers are correct in a moment. I just want to touch on two letters — **q** and **x**. The **q** is always pronounced "**k**," so it's a 7. The **x** is transposed to a number according to how it's sounded in a particular word. Example: The **x** is pronounced "**gs**" in "egsample," so it transposes to 70. That's usually the case. Not in "anxious," however; that's "an**kshi**ous" — the **x** transposes to 76. Don't worry about it; you won't be using **q** or **x**.

Make sure you've got these right:

printer = 94214	aggravate = 7481
desk = 107	clearing = 75427
collar = 754	ashen = 62
tenement = 12321	placed = 9501
crayon = 742	special = 0965
elbow = 59	gigantic = 67217
Lorayne = 542	silliness = 0520

All right; you've just acquired the basic tool for remembering numbers. I don't mean to use this as a cliff-hanger, but I have no choice. There's a thing or two I have to teach you before I can really show you how to apply this idea, how to memorize numbers, of any kind and of any length. I'll soon cover that "thing or two," but don't you "lose" the Phonetic Number/Alphabet. It's much too important. *Set* it into your mind, practice it. It's easy; you don't have to take "time out" in order to practice. When you see a word or phrase on a billboard or sign, mentally transpose it to digits. And vice versa. When you see a number (perhaps on a license plate), mentally tranpose the digits to sounds. Before you know it you'll be doing this as if you've done it all your life. The digits/sounds will be *locked in.* In the meantime . . .

Evan R. Bell *(Partner, Cogan Bell and Company):* A person with a fabulous memory makes herself or himself more indispensable to me. Of course, that person is also very capable. Difficult to separate the two things. With occasional exceptions, I find that people with exceptional memories are also quite capable.

Arlie Lazarus *(President and COO, Jamesway Corporation):* Wipe away memory and there *is* no experience.

Peter Kougasian *(Assistant District Attorney, Director of Legal Staff Training, Manhattan, New York):* The difference between an effective professional, effective executive, and a noneffective professional is that effective professionals *do not forget.* . . .

If a person in my office kept forgetting, that person wouldn't go very far. We can't accept forgetting because that person would not be professional; nonprofessionals do not do their jobs properly — and that wastes *money.*

7

No Paper!
Your Mind Is
Your Daily Planner

J ust about every executive considers it important to know exactly
what he or she has to accomplish during a particular day —
today or tomorrow.

Harvey Leeds *(Vice President of Promotion, Epic Records,
division of CBS):* Remembering things to do each business day?
That's a large part of the lifeblood of my position. That's so for all
the executives I know.

Evan R. Bell *(Partner; Cogan Bell and Company, financial
management):* Yes, it's vital that I remember things to do. I write
'em down.

HL: What if you lost that paper?
ERB: I'd be out of business!

Mel Brooks: If I'm supposed to call, say, a Mr. Carpenter — a money man, a backer — who has his checkbook ready, and I forget to call, it's possible I've given him too much time to think. He may change his mind. You simply don't forget to make a phone call in that position. You've got one shot.

Some of the executives I interviewed were not aware of the fact that errands and appointments *can* be remembered, and that pieces of paper aren't really necessary (except as backups, perhaps).

Peter Kougasian: Boy, I'm like the fellow who sets four alarm clocks. I write my errands in my pocket diary, and in my desk diary, and my secretary reminds me, and so on. I don't want to forget any. If I could remember daily things to do, confidently and definitely, that'd be fantastic — a lifesaver!

You can remember errands and appointments by *number* — in other words, so you'd know the fourth thing you want to take care of tomorrow (or today), and the eighth thing, and so on. You can remember *daily* or *weekly* appointments; that is, you can remember appointments by the hour (*today*) or by day and hour (all *week*). I'll ultimately teach you how to do all that, of course, but before you can swim you've got to get into the water. So right now, I'll show you the easiest way to remember various unnumbered things you want to do *tomorrow*.

Philip A. Bossert of *Business Week* told me that he usually has "about six things to do each business day. I'd love to be able just to remember them rather than put them on paper. I also number them; I want to remember them in order, or sequence. I always list what I have to do the next day on the night before." I assured him that I could teach him to remember *unlimited* errands per day, in order or by number, and asked him what he would think of that. Said he: "I'd feel I can walk on water!"

If you feel even a little bit like that you'll appreciate this! Let me invent a list of things you may need to do, at the office and outside of the office. I'll use only tangible objects for this list. But each will bring to mind an errand. For example, if I told you to think "hotel," it'd be because one of the things you must do tomorrow is arrange for a conference room at a certain hotel. I'm assuming that you really *know* what you have to do — you just need *reminders.* Here's your list:

book (pick up particular one)
radio (discuss planned radio commercials with advertising
    agency)
accountant (meet with accounting personnel)
airplane (order airline tickets for business trip)
carpenter (must call Mr. Jason Carpenter)
dentist (mustn't forget dental appointment)
gift (send to hostess)
hotel (arrange for conference)
speech (must do research for planned speech)
telephone (check estimates for new office telephone system —
    decision due today)

HL: Ralph, what's your trick to help you remember things to do tomorrow?
Ralph Destino: I write them down on these little pieces of paper and stick them on my mirror at home. In the morning, I'm knotting my tie in that mirror. There they are. One problem, though. I've missed a thing or two to do occasionally because two of those pieces of paper were stuck one on the other in my mirror — I saw only one of the two.

Throw away the pieces of paper. They're not needed! Let's *remember* these ten errands *in sequence.* You won't necessarily *do* them in sequence, nor have they necessarily come to mind in any particular order, but let's remember them in sequence. Begin by visualizing a book. That is, *see* a book in your mind's eye.
New information is remembered by connecting it to something you already know. My rule: **In order to remember a new thing, you**

must associate it, *in some ridiculous way,* with something you already know/remember. We'll assume that you already know/remember *book.* We'll start applying the rule of association with the next item — *radio.* What you want to accomplish is to force the thing you already know (book) to *remind you* of the new thing (radio). Form a silly, ridiculous, bizarre, *impossible* image or picture in your mind — *imagine* it — connecting those two, and *only* those two, things.

Do *not* form a logical picture. A book lying near or on a radio is too mundane, everyday, logical. It is exactly the sort of thing we *don't* remember. It doesn't *slap your face.* If you see yourself turning on a radio and having millions of books fly out of it and hit you — *that'll* slap your face. If you turn a knob on a gigantic book and music comes blaring out because it's a radio — that'll slap your face. And so will opening a book only to have radios fly out.

I'll suggest two or three pictures for each *entity of two,* but you need only one, and the technique works *much* better if you think of the image yourself. Then you'll be forcing yourself to concentrate on those two things as you never did before, and without pain. Right now, though, I have no choice but to make the suggestions. Select one of the silly pictures, or one you think of yourself and — here's the most important step — be sure you *really see* it in your mind. See it for at least a split second, then stop trying. That's book to radio.

Next, associate radio (don't use book now — that's done) to accountant, or anything that'll remind you of accountant. You might see many radios (*millions* of an item helps to make your picture crazy, impossible) bent over their desks, working on the corporate books. Or see your accountant writing numbers on a *gigantic* radio. (Imagining things as larger than life also helps to form an impossible picture.) Or, you're *count*ing radios. Select the image you think is most ridiculous or one you thought of yourself. *See it* — really. Radio and accountant.

Accountant must now remind you of airplane. Airplanes (many) are doing the books, or millions of accountants are boarding a plane, or you're *count*ing lots of airplanes. You can visualize the same basic picture as for the preceding, but with *airplane*(s) now. Select and *see.* Accountant and airplane.

Airplane to carpenter. Beware of logic: A carpenter working on a plane is *not* impossible or ridiculous. But an airplane sawing wood, hammering nails, is. You could also see a carpenter flying (spreading his arms) *instead of* an airplane. (See one item doing what the other should do.) Airplane and carpenter.

Carpenter to dentist. Almost obvious. A carpenter is working on your teeth — with hammer, chisel, saw, and so on. Or see your dentist being a carpenter (building a tooth in your mouth). Incorporating *action* is another aid for forming silly pictures. Use either image, or one you thought of, and *see it*. Carpenter and dentist.

Easy, isn't it? And it doesn't matter *how many* errands there are. Let's do the rest. Dentist has to remind you of gift. See your dentist pulling a gift out of your mouth! If you usually send flowers, he's pulling out a gigantic bouquet. Or see a large gift *being* a dentist, working on you. *See* one picture. Dentist and gift.

Gift to hotel. Bouquets of flowers, gifts, are sitting around a conference table, or entering a hotel. Or you're giving someone a gift of a hotel. Visualize it wrapped with ribbons. *See it*. Gift and hotel.

Hotel to speech. A gigantic hotel is making a speech — or you're delivering a speech to an audience consisting of hotels!

The illogical, silly pictures come to mind easily. But I want you to *think* of them a little bit, apply a *bit* of effort — that's what forces the concentration. That, and *seeing* the picture you select. Right now, see your picture of hotel and speech.

Speech to telephone. A gigantic telephone is making a speech. Or a man making a speech is flying out of your telephone as you pick it up. Speech and telephone.

If you've *seen* all the pictures, you're in for a pleasant surprise — or shock. Think of *book* (if at any time that first item doesn't come to mind right away, just think of *any* item and work *backward*), and that must remind you of . . . what? Radio, of course. Try it on your own — all the way to the end.

Did you get 'em all? If you had trouble with one or two, it was only because your picture for that wasn't silly enough or, more likely, you didn't really *see* it in your mind. So go back and change the picture or *see it clearly* or do both. You'll even know them backward!

You have formed a *Link* of those errands — you have *Linked* them. This is the Link System of memory. It is used to help remember *sequential* information.

Practically speaking, you should form the Link the night before —
as the errands come to mind. In the morning, go over the Link
mentally. It takes no time, because you do it while you're doing
something else — having your coffee, exercising, showering, shaving,
dressing. If another errand comes to mind, add it on to the Link —
associate it to the last item, that's all. During the rest of the day, simply
go over the Link every once in a while. Do the errand that's
convenient, and so on, until you're through.

With this system, there's no way you can "forget" even one of the
things you have to do. You may decide not to do it today (add it to
tomorrow's Link, or start tomorrow's Link with it), but you won't
forget it. Go over the Link before you leave for home, just to be sure
you've accomplished everything.

I've told you that I'll mention how to remember specific appointments, but I know that for many executives this simple Link technique
serves the purpose admirably. You can use the Link System for many
things: for sequential pieces of information that you don't need to
retain, like this one-day errand list, which will be wiped out as you
Link your errands for another day, and for pieces of information, lists,
that you *do* want to retain — if not forever, perhaps for a week, month,
or a year. *Retention is set by use* — the more often you *use* the
information, the longer you'll retain it, of course. (You might want to
teach the technique to your spouse; it may be used, quite effectively,
to remember a shopping list.)

> **Bernadette Skubly-Butts** *(Account Executive, Air France):* For-
> getting things to do, in my business? Like I got a letter from a VIP,
> I mean a *VIP*, requesting a ticket on the Concorde. I dropped the
> letter on my desk, and proceeded to forget to take care of it. I
> remembered just in time — the day before he had to fly. I could
> have lost a very, very, important account. Teach me, show me,
> help me!

I just did!

Before you continue reading, and learning, please turn back to chapter
4 and take Test 1 again. It's important to you, and to me, that you do

so. I want you to compare scores — before and after. Then, you can make up and try to remember some lists for practice. But the best practice is to start *using* the technique, on the job, *now*.

Some important points: Understand that actually forming a Link in your mind takes a *fraction* of the time it takes me to teach you how to do it. Once you get into the swing of it, you'll do it faster than you can write out a list, although speed is not necessarily a factor. The pictures you see in your mind will evaporate as the information becomes *knowledge;* by the third or fourth time you've *used* the information, the associations are no longer necessary. They are simply a *means to an end*. That's why you can make *as many Links as you want to or need to*.

There are many ways to use the Link System in business; I'll touch on a few later. The following usage, for lawyers, will give you a sense of the wide applicability of this technique. Herald Price Fahringer is one of the best-known trial attorneys in New York. He defended socialite Claus von Bulow during the first of von Bulow's widely publicized murder trials. In Fahringer's opinion, jury selection is the most important part of a criminal trial. In an article on this subject in the *New York Law Journal,* he lists the "topics of inquiry" that an attorney should know and pursue in order "to gain the necessary knowledge to make an enlightened choice." He talks of having a written list but adds: "On the other hand, to be effective . . . counsel should try to avoid the use of notes. Being 'pad bound' is distracting. A good trial lawyer wants to establish a great deal of eye contact with the jurors." Fahringer then suggests employing my *Link System*. He uses it.

I've selected nine of his "topics of inquiry" to show how the Link method works with this kind of information. When selecting a jury, you want to know about each juror's *family* background and circumstances: spouse's occupation, number of children, their age and sex. You want to know his *occupation:* how much authority he has, how many positions held in the past. *Education:* high school, college, degrees, which schools. Does he have a *relationship* with any law enforcement agencies? So far, if I were forming a list/Link, I'd have culled from these larger questions four points of reference: family, occupation, education, and relationship (you may prefer to use "law enforcement" here, or, preferably, a *relation* who is a law enforcer), because each word brings the whole *thought* to mind. That's all I'd need. Let's continue.

Publicity: What newspapers and magazines does he read? How much has he read or heard about the case? And another topic: Has the juror ever been the victim of a *crime?* You'll also want to know about prior *jury* service, if any. Criminal or civil case? What are the potential juror's *hobbies?* How does he spend his leisure time? Favorite television show? Has he done any *military* service? Branch, rank, combat?

Fahringer's list contains more topics of inquiry, of course, and even so, he says that it is by no means complete. Topics are added to the list, or taken from it, to meet the specific needs of each particular case. I'll show you how to Link these nine; exactly the same technique is used to Link any number of concepts. Here's the list of *reminders:*

    family, occupation, education, relationship, publicity,
    crime, jury, hobbies, military

Form a Link exactly as you've just learned to do with concrete, distinct, items. Now you're working with *concepts,* but they too evoke images — and that's what's important. All you have to do is focus on the visual image that each conjures up in *your* mind.

I wanted "family" to remind me of "occupation." So I visualized people who looked exactly alike (*family*) being *occupied.* They were all busy, paying no attention to each other. (Work along with me for practice.) "Occupation" must remind me of "education." Form a completely separate association. People of all different *occupations* — see hardhats, painters, white-collar workers, and so forth — sitting in a schoolroom being students (*education*). See that picture.

Education to *relationship* with any law enforcement agency. Imagine many policemen (law enforcement) rushing into the schoolroom and hugging, kissing, the students — because they're *relations.* See that silly picture.

Relationship to *publicity.* See your relations being interviewed by newspaper reporters. If you don't want to visualize your own relations, use the police, since they represented relations in your last association. Or see your relations (real or police) reading lots of newspapers and magazines. Your choice — but *see* it, and you already know the first few topics of inquiry.

Publicity to *crime*. See many thieves stealing reporters' cameras and notebooks. Thieves = crime; reporters = publicity. *Crime* to prior *jury* service. A crime is being committed in the *jury* box, against all the jurors, at the same time. Or twelve murderers are sitting in the box — they *are* the jury.

Jury to *hobbies*. All members of the jury are collecting stamps, participating in other *hobbies* — paying no attention to counsel, witnesses, or judge. *Hobbies* to *military*. You might see millions of gigantic stamps (*hobby*) carrying rifles, marching off to war (*military*).

If you were using this technique as Fahringer does, as you interrogated the juror, one topic would automatically lead to the next. Even if you were interrupted, for any reason, you would be able to get right back into your Link. Stop for a moment; see if you know all the topics.

I want you to see that you can Link and therefore remember concepts such as these topics of inquiry. Apply exactly the same techniques to help you remember, say, the questions you want to ask during a business negotiation: When can this contract go into effect? Will the deal be worldwide? What percentage of the agreed-upon money changes hands on signing? Can we have at least two of our own people closely involved at all times? And so forth. The technique can also be used by doctors to remember the list of questions to be asked during a patient's physical checkup. Do you have any allergies? Does anyone in your family have allergies? Are you on any medication? Do you smoke? Drink? When did you last have a complete physical? And more, of course.

The Link method of memory is a strong weapon to use in your battle against "forgetting"!

J. K. Hartman *(Managing Director and CEO, Scudder, Stevens and Clark, investment counselors):* Our business has two hats — one is the investment stuff, the other is the client side. Both sides are heavily rooted in memory. We think of people like Bernard Baruch and John Templeton as having the "nose," a "smell" — having intuitive skills, hunches. It boils down to *memory*. They remembered facts. It's all experience, knowledge, memory — an associative process. They think of a stock or industry and long histories of industry movements, special ratios, how it does in up and down markets, and much more flashes through their minds. It's all associative; that's why memory is really the key to their seeming intuitive or genius response. You have to remember the history before you can come up with an "intuitive" response.

HL: So without memory you couldn't really advise a client properly — you'd be shooting fish in a barrel.

JKH: Sure. The difference between an unseasoned beginner and one who's been through it is the buildup of the memory bank, experience. To apply *any* analysis to the stock market, you *must* remember the history of the stock market.

8

Memory Makes for Effective Time Management

Remember to Save Time in Business by Spending It Wisely

I've read it in every book on achieving business success — the "million-dollar idea" for managing time: Don't let a piece of paper go through your hands more than once. That is, handle it, delegate it, throw it away. Well, that's a pretty good timesaving idea, but the truth is, it's actually more of a *memory aid* than anything else. You see, too often it's when you drop that piece of paper somewhere on your desk, thinking, "I'll take care of it later or tomorrow," that you forget about it. You may come across it a week or a month later and it's the smack-palm-on-forehead moment: "Damn! I forgot all about this."

The "million-dollar idea" is really the do-it-now concept. *Do it;* that way you can't forget it — it's *done.* I asked a few executives whether they agreed that the handle-it-only-once idea was really a memory aid, and a very *good* one at that.

J. K. Hartman: The million-dollar idea. Sure. It's an oversimplification, of course, but I agree that it's a memory aid. Thinking you'll do it later is the killer. That's when you forget it. And one of the biggest infringers, offenders, and negators of time management is forgetting!

William Seco *(Vice President of Sales and Engineering, EDP World, Inc.):* Of course. And the more time my people can save by remembering things — not forgetting — the more money they can make.

Doing it *at that moment* is a great time-saver — because it eliminates forgetting. It's the put-it-into-your-briefcase-*right-now* rule. Go into a Sloppy Joe diner during lunch hour. Watch the short-order cook use time effectively: No matter what order the waiter calls, the cook immediately takes out one key ingredient that will *remind* him of that order. That's a double-edger; it's a do-it-at-that-moment trick that doesn't *allow* forgetting! Think about it. That strip of bacon *instantly* tossed onto the grill is much better than the proverbial string around your finger, because the string will only remind you that you wanted to remember *something*. The strip of bacon reminds the short-order cook of a bacon, lettuce, and tomato sandwich!

Richard Schlott *(President, Schlott Realtors — 150 offices, 6,000 employees):* Every top executive I know is *always* in a time bind — feels he can't possibly get it all done — *always*. Sure, that million-dollar time idea is really an aid to *remembering*. Absolutely; leave it for later and it's forgotten.

Plutarch wrote that "the greatest of all sacrifices is the sacrifice of time." There's no question that this is the one area where we're all equal. Each minute contains sixty seconds, every hour consists of sixty minutes, and every day is made up of twenty-four hours, no matter who is using that minute, hour, or day. No matter who you are or who you know, there's no way to squeeze an extra second, minute, or hour into that minute, hour, or day. So, the only way to gain or *save* time is to *spend* it wisely, to use it *effectively*.

One time-saver that everyone I interviewed agreed on is planning your day. In many cases, of course, that's automatic — your day is filled with appointments, perhaps. Fine. But if it isn't, if that's not the way your business operates, plan your day. I've already given you help in that department. Form a Link that *tells* you the things you must do today — the daily planner in your mind! Forming that Link does three things for you:

1. It enables you to remember the things to do.
2. It *forces* you to plan your day; just thinking of all those things to do begins the planning for you.
3. It's a *commitment*. The act of forming the Link implies that you are committing yourself to that plan.

I learned an interesting rule from a few executives I interviewed for this book. It's the "80-20 rule." In most businesses, 80 percent of the accounts receivable are from 20 percent of the clients.

That 80-20 rule applies to quite a few areas, including time management. It's easy enough to memorize, say, twenty-five things to do tomorrow now that you know how to form a Link. The problem is, there's no way you'll make the time to do them all. The 80-20 rule is sometimes referred to as the *vital few/trivial many* concept. Cull out the trivial many, keep the vital few on your list — plan properly — and you'll save *time*.

Stick to your plan for the day as closely as you can and you're probably using time effectively. Of course, you know that you must leave some unscheduled time in your plan, for relaxation and for emergencies that have a habit of arising. (Every time you make plans, *life* happens!) But while some flexibility within your plan is necessary, *unlimited* flexibility is a time-waster. Using the Link should both organize your time more efficiently *and* act as a motivator.

There's more. It's difficult to plan the things to do in a day without deciding what your goals are for that day. So in making a Link you're forced, without realizing it, to do that, too — to get your goals clear in your mind. Once those goals are clear, the plan becomes a list of *actions* that will lead to the attainment of those goals. Planning to meet those goals by doing certain things within a specified time frame is good time management.

I follow another time-saving subrule, which may just be the antithesis of yours, and, again, it's also a *memory* aid. Under most circumstances I do the things that can wait *first,* then I do the urgent ones! You see, the *urgent* things are — well — urgent; they get done *because* they're urgent; you *have* to take care of them, and those are never *forgotten* — they're too *urgent!* It's those chores that can wait that usually *do* wait and wait, and linger, and cause aggravation and indecision, and *waste time* because you don't get to them for one reason or another. One of those reasons is that you *forget* them. When you know there are urgent duties waiting, it's amazing how quickly the minor decisions are made, and the things that "can wait" get done!

Make it a habit to start things *on time.* That habit alone can save you hundreds of hours a year. Make up your mind to start on time, and it becomes habit. It's the "laters" that do you in: most "laters" are forgotten, and *forgetting wastes time!*

Another simple time-saving truth: Most everything takes more time than you think it will. Leave yourself *cushions* of time, to take care of that. If you think you can handle a particular chore in half an hour, schedule forty-five minutes. You can't lose. If it takes forty-five minutes, you've scheduled for it. If it takes less time, *do something else,* something you'd have had to keep until tomorrow. (I don't read the six-month-old magazines in doctors' offices — I bring *work* with me. I'm sure I've written at least two books during flying time, train time, waiting in offices, airports, and on-lines time. It's a great feeling, too. I haven't *wasted* time, nor have I let delays or other people's inefficiency waste it for me. It's *my* time!)

And when the boss asks you to do something, just try saying either, "If I remember," or "If I have the time." If he or she is anything like me — and those I interviewed are — you'll hear "Just *do* it," or something that means exactly that.

That's my number-one time-saving device, advice, remark, cliché: **Just *do* it!**

HL: Richard, what's important to remember when you're an architect?

Richard Roth, Jr. *(President, Emery Roth and Sons, architects — the firm that helped design the World Trade Center, the Pan Am Building, and the Citicorp Building, among others):* [After a long silence.] The reason I haven't answered you yet is because memory is important in just about *every* area in this business. Besides the normal "people" things like remembering names, faces, phone numbers, appointments, and so forth, architects have to remember blueprints, differences in edifices, building codes and landmark dos and don'ts in different cities, "ball-park" contractor, service, and supply prices, and so much more.

You also asked about forgetting. Generally speaking, the person who forgets is too often worthless. The person who has a great memory, in *all* areas, has made himself indispensable to us.

9

Decision Making/ Problem Solving/ Memory

A Key Component in the Success Equation

Sometimes I find it awfully difficult to decide what to order when I'm dining out! (Even though I've usually memorized the entire menu.) My wife and guests squirm impatiently as I struggle to make that decision. My excuse is, "Gimme a break; when I write, *every word* is a decision! I've made thousands of decisions today, so it's difficult to make one when I'm not working — not writing." This is usually said half facetiously. I found out, via the interviews for this book, that most CEOs view their lives as being equally decision-filled. They spend their days, and perhaps nights, making business decisions and solving business problems (and then can't decide what to eat!).

Ralph Destino: I couldn't make business decisions without my memory. I don't like to agonize over decisions. I make them quickly. I make them instinctively. What allows them to be instinctive? It's a direct outflow from memory. It's fundamental — all the things I remember help me make those "instinctive" decisions.

I've heard it said that Lee Iacocca makes snap decisions — too quickly. Well, because of his memory, his vast body of knowledge, he can do that. He's usually right!

HL: As we've agreed, everyone in a managerial position is a decision maker. You too.
Cy Leslie: Every hour of every day. The more I remember about a situation, the faster and better each decision can be made. It's a store of information that's absolutely vital in making my decision. To know, to commit to memory, to be able to pull out of memory is *very* vital.

Interesting — when my secretary told me that you had called to interview me, Harry, I *remembered* that we'd done some business together twenty-six years ago. I remembered you kindly, in a good sense. That memory helped me make the instant decision to see you.

All executives are decision makers and problem solvers. There are rules, dos and don'ts, to aid the executive in making decisions and solving problems. It's difficult, sometimes, to separate those two areas. The basic difference between the two is that in decision making there is usually a *choice* whereas in problem solving there must be a *solution*. A few of my interviewees used almost the same words when they described the importance of memory in these areas. **Peter Kougasian** must make decisions in his work. "Without memory," he said, "how could I make them intelligently? I couldn't. The more I remember, the more intelligent, and usually right, is my decision." And **Philip A. Bossert** said, "You have to remember all the facts. The more facts you remember, the more intelligent your decision will be — the better and faster your solution to a problem."

Of course. It's important for us to remember what occurred in the *past* in order to make a decision in the *present* that's going to be used in the *future*.

There is a theory you should know about. Most of the executives I interviewed did not know about it. It's the *minimax theory.*

Dueling with pistols — ten paces, turn, and fire — is what gave birth to the *minimax* theory. The duelists, pistols in hand, stand back to back, then walk away from each other counting off ten paces — then whirl and fire. It would seem that the best thing to do would be to whirl and fire rapidly, before the other person does. But wait. Each person has only one bullet in his pistol. What if you whirl, fire quickly — and miss?

You haven't solved a problem, you've created one. You've enabled your opponent to take the time to *aim* and fire. Well then, what's the right thing to do — let your opponent shoot first, hope he misses, and then take *your* time to aim and fire? But what if *he* doesn't miss? What if he has second-guessed you? He believes you intend to let him fire first, so *he'll* take his time to aim before he fires.

Is a puzzlement!

Theoretically, it's best to whirl and fire — but to do so at the *proper instant.* That instant is the one split second where chance of failure (missing) is at its *mini*mum and chance for success (scoring a hit) is at its *maxi*mum. *That's* the instant during which to fire; that's the *minimax* instant. When exactly *is* that instant? I don't know, and I don't think you'll get the answer from anyone but a great duelist! The answer would entail thorough *knowledge* of the entire situation. The facts you *remember* would help toward pinpointing that elusive instant: Is your opponent an experienced duelist? Has he dueled before and won? Was he ever wounded? Is he a hunter, or is he afraid of the sport? What's the rate of speed of your whirl? His whirl? How does your marksmanship rate? His marksmanship? And so on.

It's nice that you will probably never have to decide when to fire at an opponent. But we do make business decisions every day. Be aware of the minimax theory when making these decisions, because there is always, in every situation, that one fleeting instant within which you have the minimum chance of failure and the maximum chance for success. That "fleeting instant" could be as short as a moment or as long as a month. But just *knowing* that the minimax instant exists and that *memory* is a great help toward pinpointing it will make you reach for it with more awareness, and perhaps more success. Bear it in mind and you'll be a better decision-maker: you will eventually know just when to pull the trigger! As **Joseph V. Casale** said to me during our interview, "Making intelligent decisions is my business, my profession. Without memory it's a gamble."

Thinking in the past is remembering; thinking in the present is often problem solving, decision making. (Thinking in the future is anticipating.) Now, a few quick problem-solving rules; memory is a large part of the second rule, but first things first. The first rule for problem solving is: **Define the problem precisely** — "precisely" meaning to weed out the unessential incidentals. List only the essentials of the problem — exactly *what* is wrong, *where* it is wrong, and, if you can find out, *why* it's wrong. Most problems precisely defined are already partially solved. And in some instances, when you can find out exactly *what's* wrong and *why*, the problem is solved.

If not, list all the obstacles standing in the way of solution. Beside each obstacle note any and all solutions for just that individual obstacle, no matter how farfetched. Use my memory systems to memorize these obstacles/solutions, if you like, and you'll be accelerating toward the decision-making moment (perhaps the "*minimax*" moment) — the solution to the main problem — at top speed.

What you've done is search out the *core* problem within the overall problem; you're ready to attack the octopus, not just its tentacles. I remember being told by a student of mine who designed bridges that the actual construction of a bridge is not usually the core problem, nor is that the matter about which most of the decisions have to be made. Foreseeing the traffic is the main problem. Deciding, judging, such things as where most of the traffic will be coming from and where it will be going is key. How heavy will it be at peak hours, and how much heavier will it get in the future? The *traffic* is the core problem, not the bridge itself. As always, *remembering* past similar situations would help to find the *core* problem and get to the answers to these questions *faster*.

The second rule: **Know the facts you need to solve that problem.** That means *remember* them. Facts are the essential tools for any kind of thinking, certainly for decision making or problem solving. That's where memory comes in, of course. The more facts you remember about any specific problem, the easier it is to solve. But if you don't remember enough facts, you'd better know where and how to *get* them. Gather as much information as you can — within a reasonable span of time. Waiting to get every *possible* fact is too close to indecision. The *cost* of information must also be taken into consideration.

> **Scott Marcus:** There's absolutely no question that memory is important in decision making. The ability to remember similar situations and experiences is crucial. That holds for problem solving, too.

When you feel you know all the facts, apply the third rule: **Keep an open mind and weigh all sides of the problem.** The first step should be to ask yourself: How in the world did we allow this to happen? Who or what got us into this predicament? *Why* did this *become* a problem in the first place? Find the *causes*.

Then, again, your experience, your *memory,* comes into play. *Thinking clearly* is what it boils down to. Consider, weigh, each aspect of the problem and then, apply the fourth rule: **Let your thoughts lead to action.** In order to, figuratively speaking, GOYA (get off your ass), determine what the outcome of your thinking should be. Try to visualize what solution/decision is best for the firm. How soon would you *actually* want to see action taken? Within what budget? How much risk are you willing to accept? Who should you assign to handle it? Then — *act*.

So, the decision-making, problem-solving rules and subrules:

1. Define the problem precisely.
  • Get to the core of that problem.

2. Know the facts you need to solve that problem.
  • Gather all the information you can pertaining to the problem.

3. Keep an open mind and weigh all sides of the problem.
  • How and why was the problem caused?
  • Who or what caused it?

4. Let your thoughts lead to action.
   • Visualize what you'd like the outcome to be.
   • Make your decision, reach your solution — and *act* on it.

Your intuition, instinct, and *experience* will come to bear throughout this process. To me, and to all the top-level executives I discussed it with, there can *be* no intuition or experience (and probably no instinct) without *memory*.

HL: What qualifications are needed to be successful in your business?
William Seco *(Vice President of Sales and Engineering, EDP World, Inc.):* Aside from the ability to establish credibility and salesmanship and all that good stuff, memory is very important. I was promoted to my position because of who and what I remember. Wipe out my memory and I couldn't hold this position. If I can't remember the computer executives I have available, what their qualifications are, on which computers they're expert, which firms need executives with what expertise — what good am I? Without my memory, the company doesn't need me!
HL: Are you saying that if a new person in a similar company could remember fairly rapidly the things *you* already know, he or she would reach your position?
WS: Sure. And we're an information business. It's okay to say, "I'll look it up," but only a couple of times. You'd better remember the answers.
HL: Has forgetting anything ever cost you an opportunity?
WS: Oh, sure.
HL: Can you tell me what?
WS: I forgot!

10

Continue Making Numbers Easy to Remember

Juggle Them as Never Before

A few chapters back, you made a Link of ten things to do during your business day. You remembered the ten things in sequence only. Most likely, you still remember that practice list. But if I asked you right now, "What is the sixth errand on that list?" could you tell me instantly? Without counting on your fingers? I don't think so; you *must* count to it in order to know its numerical position. That's okay; knowing them in sequence is *computerlike*. But, in this chapter, we'll eliminate the *"like"* — and really make your mind work *better* than a computer!

Harvey Leeds: Being able to remember well is essential in my business. There are other essential areas, but memory has to be way up there.

Harry Lorayne: I know you have to remember telephone numbers, which radio station call letters go with which city, and the names of program or music directors at specific radio stations.

Leeds: And appointments.

Lorayne: You said something that interested me in that regard. You said that when you write down things to do for each business day, you find it "sets" more firmly in your mind if you list them by *number*.

Leeds: Yeah; I don't know exactly why. I don't necessarily handle them in that numerical order. But for me writing reinforces remembering for certain information.

Lorayne: That's good. You use writing as an aid to memory, not as a *substitute* for it. Many executives tell me the same thing. But what would happen if you lost or misplaced that paper?

Leeds: I'd remember a lot of the things to do. Those I'd forget would cause aggravation.

You'll eliminate that aggravation if you simply remember the information. And you do *not* have to write any data next to the numbers 1 to 10 in order to know that data from number 1 to 10. No, you don't! Back, then, to numbers and the Phonetic Number/Alphabet. Think of your (or any) *tie* — a man's *tie* — and that will *tell* you what the *first* thing is. There is only one consonant sound in the word "tie," and that one consonant sound (**t**) can represent only one digit: 1. So, if you see yourself wearing a *bicycle* around your neck *instead of* a tie, or a bicycle wearing a tie, or a gigantic tie riding a bicycle, that would *tell* you that the number-one thing you have to do tomorrow is, say, check on that shipment of bicycles!

You could also use other words: **t**ea, ai**d**, **d**ye, **t**oe, a**d**e, **h**a**t**, a**t**e, **h**o**t**, and so on. Seeing any one of them in your mind would work as well. I've selected the words I think are easiest to visualize, and easiest to fit into associations. Obviously, a *thing* can be visualized; abstract numbers *cannot*. But it's basically an arbitrary selection on my part. I'll be teaching you the *Peg Words* (that's what I call them) that I've used to represent numbers for many years. And let me anticipate a question. Yes, you can choose a word to represent *any* number *when you need it,* and you may end up doing just that with larger numbers. But it's important at the start simply to know a Peg Word for smaller numbers. Then, they'll *be there,* ready to work for you *instantly.*

I'm not advocating or using rote memory. If I gave you *any* ten words, that'd be rote, but that's not the case here. The Peg Words must follow the simple pattern of containing the proper consonant sounds. Look:

1. tie		6. shoe
2. Noah		7. cow
3. ma		8. ivy
4. rye		9. bee
5. law		10. toes

Go over them; be sure you understand *why* each one can represent only its specific digit. And form a basic picture for each. For *Noah,* I picture a long, gray beard (he was an *old* man) or an ark. *Rye* can be whiskey or bread; *law* can be a cop, a judge, or a judge's gavel; *ivy* is a green plant that grows on walls. It's what *you* see in your mind that counts.

The first nine Peg Words each contain only one consonant sound because they each represent a *one*-digit number. *Toes* contains two consonant sounds; 10 is a *two*-digit number. There's that simple substitution concept again.

I want you to *know* these ten Peg Words. If you know the sounds, you probably already *do* know the words. Something additional to bear in mind: all the concepts, all the techniques I'm teaching you are being used to solve one specific memory problem at the time of teaching. It's the only way to teach them. But all the techniques eventually *blend,* work *together,* to solve all memory problems. That's why you can't bypass any part of the techniques. Each is a stepping-stone to a higher, more important, plateau. Right now, knowing the ten sounds of the Phonetic Number/Alphabet (in any order) makes it a snap also to know the ten Peg Words. Go over them for a few minutes. Then, fill in these blanks as a simple drill; do it fairly rapidly.

1 is _Tie_   8 is _Cow_   cow is no. _9_   2 is _Norold_

rye is no. _4_   9 is _____   ivy is no. _6_   3 is _MO_

5 is _K_   10 is _Toes_   bee is no. _9_   6 is _Shoa_

4 is _Ry_   7 is _____   6 is _Shoe_   tie is no. _1_

toes is no. _10_   law is no. _5_   1 is _Tie_   Noah is no. _2_

3 is _MO_   8 is _Bee_   ma is no. _3_   shoe is no. _6_

1 is _Tie_   2 is _Noent_   3 is _MO_   4 is _Rye_

5 is _Law_   10 is _Toe_   9 is _____   8 is _Bee_

7 is _Be_   6 is _Shoe_   5 is _Law_   4 is _Ry_

You got 'em!

Now, you're wondering: So what? Why do I need those words?

You've just made a deposit in your memory bank. Probably the most *important* deposit you'll ever make. The "principal" will always remain in your account; you'll live off the interest for the rest of your life. You'll want to show your spouse, friends, children, business acquaintances, relatives, employees, how to make the same deposit in *their* memory banks! Have I made it seem important enough to you?

And are you now wondering how much more you have to learn to know/remember/memorize things by number? Nothing. You already know all you need to know. Just *work along* with me — that's *essential*.

The sixth item on tomorrow's agenda is to arrange to buy 500,000 envelopes for the spring mailing. "Envelope" is all you need as the *reminder*. Well, let me lay out the problem, specifically. You can visualize an envelope, no problem there. But how in the world do you visualize 6? Ordinarily, you really couldn't. But *now* — I've been teaching the idea for decades, and it still excites me — you *can* picture 6. Because you have a word — your Peg Word — that *represents* 6, *means* 6, is *the same as* 6!

I told you that in order to remember to an unparalleled degree, you must learn to make intangibles tangible. Now you've done it! The number 6 is intangible to almost everyone, but *not to my students,* not to you. The Peg Word *shoe* is easily visualized; it's certainly *tangible* — and it's the same as 6! I've just rolled this little concept ("tasks" by number) into one tight little ball for you.

All you have to do is make an association between *two* things — and you already know how to do that. In this case, connect *shoe* to *envelope* — associate envelope and shoe. Same as you've already done — a silly, illogical, impossible picture. You're wearing envelopes instead of shoes; you're sealing a shoe and mailing it; a gigantic envelope is wearing shoes (walking). No problem thinking up an association, is there? You want *one* picture, and you can think it up yourself. (I'm not only training your memory, I'm forcing you to exercise your *imagination* and creative thinking. You're using your imagination and ingenuity — your *imaginuity*.) That's shoe to envelope.

The *third* thing you have to do tomorrow is finish negotiating with the new trucking company. *Truck* is enough to remind you of the thing to do, and your Peg Word, *ma,* is 3. Put 'em together. Not too much imagination (or time) needed; just see your mother driving an enormous truck. (Unless your mother really does drive a truck, this is a ridiculous, though not necessarily impossible, picture!) Or maybe a truck packed with hundreds of women; they all look (or *are*) your mother. *See* the silly picture. Ma/truck.

Task number 9: call your stockbroker. A gigantic *bee* is working on the floor of the stock exchange, or your stockbroker is being attacked by millions of bees. *See* bee/stockbroker.

I've already discussed the *first* thing you want to do — check on the bicycle shipment. *Tie* is number 1; associate bicycle to it, as per the examples I gave you. Tie/bicycle.

Number 8: make train reservations. Visualize, imagine, see — *think* — trains growing all over a wall like *ivy.* Or, millions of pieces of ivy are boarding a train. Don't get overconfident — *see* that picture. (You won't remember it if you don't.) Ivy/train.

The *fifth* thing to do is attend a meeting. You can see lots of policemen (*law*) breaking up a meeting. Or judges' gavels are attending a meeting. See it: law/meeting.

Number 10: straighten out the shipping-room problem. Millions of *toes* are being shipped, or *toes* are your shipping clerks. See the image you selected, or one you thought of yourself. Toes/shipping room.

Number 2: you have to arrange for more security guards. *Noah* is 2. A few long, gray beards (in uniform) are guarding your premises. Or a security guard is hiding in a man's beard, or a guard is hanging from someone's chin instead of a beard! (I don't care *how* ridiculous you get — let yourself go! The sillier the better.) See the silliness: Noah (beard)/security guards.

Number 7: plan, delegate, for the office Christmas party. A *cow* is decorating a Christmas tree; a cow is being decorated instead of a Christmas tree; you're milking a cow and Christmas ornaments come out. Cow/Christmas.

Number 4: place a magazine ad. A magazine is drinking *rye* whiskey from a bottle, magazines pour out of a whiskey bottle, a whiskey bottle is reading a magazine. Picture one of them. Rye/magazine.

I gave you the things to do in haphazard order. *Your computer memory,* the one you're cultivating at this moment, can put them into correct numerical sequence! No programming is necessary, no keys need be struck, no disks have to be put into the disk drive. Your mind, the best computer of all, simply does it — *it already has.* Check it out.

Think, merely think, *tie.* Do you see? Do I have to say anything else? Thinking *tie* made you think of bicycle.

Think of *Noah.* What does that bring to mind? Security guards! You have to hire more of them.

Think of your *ma.* That should immediately make you also think of . . . truck, and, of course, that automatically means "negotiating with the new trucking company."

Think of your Peg Word for number 4 (you should "see" *rye* immediately). Rye reminds you of . . . magazine; arrange for that full-page ad.

Number 5: the Peg Word is . . . *law.* Cops or judges' gavels make you think of . . . your meeting, of course.

Number 6 is *shoe* (this is the first example I used). What is the sixth thing you want to do? *Envelope* — arrange to buy 500,000 envelopes.

Number 7: cow. Delegate for the Christmas party.

Number 8: ivy. Let's see, what was growing on a wall like ivy? Trains. Make your train reservations.

Number 9: bee. Bees were attacking — whom? Your stockbroker. Call him.

Number 10: toes. Shipping-room problem to straighten out.

Of course you knew them all. If you didn't, think back and strengthen the weak (not-*clear*-enough) associations. But you know them better than you realize. You put them into *correct order* automatically. Now, try this test, and work for *speed.* Just fill in these twenty-four blanks as quickly as you can.

Shipping room: _____   No. 3: _____

Truck: _____   Stockbroker: _____

No. 5: _____   No. 10: _____

No. 6: _____   No. 9: _____

No. 4: _____   No. 8: _____

Bicycle: _____   No. 7: _____

Guards: _____   No. 6: _____

No. 9: _____   No. 5: _____

No. 1: _____   No. 4: _____

Christmas party: _____   No. 3: _____

Train reservations: _____   No. 2: _____

No. 7: _____   No. 1: _____

We both know that if the Peg Words were second nature, you'd have filled in the blanks as quickly as you can write. When they *are* second nature, do this drill again — see for yourself. And after you've rested, please take Test 5 again (page 29). See the progress you've made! Then, turn back to this page.

Now I want to anticipate another question: "What if I had twenty things to do?"

Sure; obvious question. Obvious answer, too. If you can form a Peg Word for 10, a two-digit number, why not form Peg Words for numbers 11 to 20? Stay within the "sound" rules, and it's easy.

11. tot	16. dish
12. tin	17. dog
13. tomb	18. dove
14. tire	19. tub
15. towel	20. nose

Go over them, and be sure you see how each one stays firmly within the Phonetic Number/Alphabet rules. When you think you know them, try to remember the following, exactly as you did with numbers 1 to 10. Each item again represents a thing to do in your business.

11. scissors	16. kaleidoscope
12. blotter	17. window
13. corrugated carton	18. transparent tape
14. rubber band	19. check
15. lamp	20. brochure

Test yourself on tasks 11 to 20. Then test yourself (or have someone you don't mind impressing do it for you) on tasks *1 to 20*. Do it in order and out of order. Think of any number and the thing to do should come to mind; think of anything to do and you'll know its numerical position. Try it.

When you use this technique in real life, form your Peg List the night before. Say your mental list contains twelve things to do. During your business day, every once in a while, go over your Peg Words, 1 to 12 — *tie* to *tin*. That's all. You'll *know* what things remain to be done!

Now, I doubt if you'll ever want to remember *100* things to do in a day. (You can if you want to.) But you may want to remember 100 *other* things by number. In any case, there'll be plenty of times when you'll want to remember a two-digit number greater than 20 — for prices, telephone numbers, specific appointments, and so much more. The best and fastest way is to have a Peg Word ready. So on page 94 I have listed the words I use from 21 to 100. Knowing the Phonetic Number/Alphabet makes it easy to learn them. Do it — you'll be glad you did.

21. net	41. rod	61. sheet	81. fit
22. nun	42. rain	62. chain	82. phone
23. name	43. ram	63. chum	83. foam
24. Nero	44. rower	64. cherry	84. fur
25. nail	45. roll	65. jail	85. file
26. notch	46. roach	66. choo-choo	86. fish
27. neck	47. rock	67. chalk	87. fog
28. knife	48. roof	68. chef	88. fife
29. knob	49. rope	69. ship	89. fob
30. mouse	50. lace	70. case	90. bus
31. mat	51. lot	71. cot	91. bat
32. moon	52. lion	72. coin	92. bone
33. mummy	53. loom	73. comb	93. bum
34. mower	54. lure	74. car	94. bear
35. mule	55. lily	75. coal	95. bell
36. match	56. leech	76. cage	96. beach
37. mug	57. log	77. coke	97. book
38. movie	58. lava	78. cave	98. puff
39. mop	59. lip	79. cob	99. pipe
40. rose	60. cheese	80. fuse	100. disease thesis

Select a mind picture for each one. Go over them a few times, and you'll have them. You'll be amazed at how handy they'll be. Once you're familiar with them, you'll have a *concrete image* to represent any two-digit number. Suppose someone at a meeting mentions that he'd like to see the file on store number 49. Immediately see yourself opening a file to find lengths of *rope* flying out! How can you forget it?

To quote Benton Love, of Texas Commerce Bancshares (*Fortune,* August 1978): "The executive who tells me he can't remember numbers tells me that he can't remember the significant part of his business and is operating on quicksand."

Finally, if you've been using the Link method to remember sequential information, you may have stumbled across one minor problem: not remembering the *first* item of a Link. Well, I did mention one simple solution when I originally taught you the Link System. If you can't think of the first item, start with any item near the top, and work backward. There's nowhere to go *but* to the first item. Another way to solve this problem would be to associate the first item to *yourself*. But now that you have a way to visualize the number 1, you can use that image to begin your Link. Simply associate the first item on any list to *tie*. When you have to use that list, that information, think "tie." That immediately tells you what the first item is — and you're off and running.

Frank V. AtLee *(Executive Vice President, American Cyanamid Corporation):* You cannot deal in today's complex business world and be effective, I think, if you don't have a good memory. In our business, you need a good memory for numbers, pharmaceutical names, people's names, and all the business details that need handling every business day. There's too much happening too quickly *not* to remember things.

HL: If I could give you a photographic memory in one area, is there one you'd select?

FVA: No. The term is "general manager" — he should have a good general memory across the board: people, facts, figures.

11

Memory Power — Pyramid Power

To recap, all my systems are based on, and perform like, *natural* phenomena. There are three main principles — with nothing "Twilight Zoney" about them; they're not ephemeral, vague thoughts. They're *definites*. They are the Reminder Principle; the Slap-in-the-Face Principle; and the principle or *fact* that what can be *visualized* is *easy to remember*. The Reminder Principle is based on that natural associative process which enables you to see or think of one thing and have that thing make you mentally snap your fingers, and say, "Oops, that *reminds* me!" — it reminds you of another, different thing. And I've been showing you that reminders can be derived from *conscious* effort instead of through an automatic (but not necessarily reliable) subconscious process.

The early Greek philosopher-teachers (Aristotle, Socrates, Simonides, Plato) would slap a student's face when they imparted an important piece of information! That made the moment (and the information) memorable. It *pinpointed* attention. I've taught you to slap yourself in the face *mentally*. That's principle two.

And Aristotle wrote, "In order to think we must speculate with images." He knew, thousands of years ago, that we must see, *visualize,* images in our minds in order to *think* and, therefore, remember.

When I told you that the way to remember a new piece of information is to associate it with something you already know or remember, I wasn't just whistling "Dixie." There was once (perhaps still is) a "pyramid" craze, which made about as much sense as believing in a Ouija board. I've told you, I'm interested in results: specifics, definites. But I *do* have my own pyramid theory. Visualize that pyramid upside down, balancing on its point, and you'll have a diagram or schematic of how knowledge, or progress, *happens*.

Knowledge (like memory, because those two magnets really can't be pulled apart) is acquired in only one way; new facts, new information, new knowledge is attached to, connected to, what we *already know*. Not until you know the alphabet and the sounds that the letters make can you read. Not until you know where the D key is on a computer keyboard, and with which finger you hit it, can you add another piece of knowledge: "The E key is *above the D key;* I can hit it with the same finger if I move that finger up one row." A *fact* is rarely in limbo; it does not stand alone.

We begin knowing very little — the narrow point of the upside-down pyramid. As information is attached to that very little bit of knowledge, the original base expands, in all directions — creating the upside-down pyramid. The older and wiser we grow, the higher and wider becomes the pyramid. If you think about what I've taught you up to now, you'll see that that's just what's been happening. You acquired *one* piece of knowledge; that enabled you to acquire another "byte" of knowledge, which enabled you to acquire another . . . and so on. *That's* "pyramid power."

New knowledge is acquired by being connected to something we already know. New "things" are remembered by being associated to something we already know.

  Same thing — same principle.

Ellen Hassman *(President, AC and R Direct, Inc., subsidiary of Ted Bates World Wide — one of the largest advertising agencies):* How can someone get ahead in my company? By being knowledgeable — that comes first. The person with a great memory will definitely come to my attention.

HL: And how about yourself where memory is concerned?

EH: I have to gather and know my own information, more so than a male executive. I have to remember everything about a client's product, advertising campaign, his likes and dislikes, all we've talked about at various meetings. He may be one of *fifty* clients that I'm juggling at the same time, but he doesn't care. So far as he's concerned, he's my *only* client. I simply *have* to remember — I'd *better* remember.

12

The Name Game

Remembering Personnel by Name
Equals Administrative Power;
Remembering Clients by Name
Equals Money-Making Power

I'd love to continue my discussion of numbers. And that'd certainly seem to be the logical thing to do. But all memory problems are entities of *two*. No matter how complicated they may seem, they break down to that. Indeed, a memory problem can't be an entity of *one*. Nothing is remembered in a vacuum; *everything* is connected to something else. The point is that before we can proceed with numbers, you have to learn how to connect that entity (a number) to *the other entity*.

What's the point of remembering a telephone number or an address if you don't remember the *name* of the person or company that the number or address belongs to? Or what's the point of knowing a style number or a stock price without knowing which product or stock it pertains to? There *is* no point. Just as, in most cases, there's no point in remembering a *name* if you don't remember the *face* it goes with! I have no choice, then, but to teach you how to visualize names (of people, places, corporations, things) before I continue with numbers. It's also important for you to learn how to handle people's names before we discuss faces.

HL: You deal with highly situated politicians. Is it important for you to remember names of politicians?

Arthur Levitt, Jr.: And of anyone else. And it's important for politicians to remember names.

HL: Quite a few use my systems. But I'm under oath not to use their names or to publicize it. I guess they don't want it known that they have good to great memories — they'd never again be able to say to an investigating committee, "I forgot," or "I don't remember"! But they are well aware of the fact — they made me aware of it years ago — that to remember a voter's name is statesmanship, to forget it is political oblivion.

AL, Jr.: Of course. I think remembering names (among other things) furthers my career to this very day. Forgetting things is, I think, very dangerous in terms of personal relationships. If you forget a person's name, you tend to diminish his importance in his own eyes and, in a people business, that's a very unfortunate characteristic.

HL: I don't know how hands-on your position is. For example, do you go down to the floor of the exchange at all?

AL, Jr.: Yes. I think that's an important part of my situation.

HL: You feel you have to be there physically?

AL, Jr.: Yes.

HL: Why?

AL, Jr.: They're my flock; they're my constituents. I serve at their pleasure. They're the people we're really working with, so I spend a lot of time making my presence known, remembering their names, acknowledging them.

HL: You said remembering a messenger's name is important to you?

Michael K. Stanton: Remembering the name of a million-dollar client is, of course, of utmost importance. But sure, so is remembering the name of the messenger boy on the thirtieth floor. That's critical in the chain of events that goes toward servicing a client. First of all, that messenger boy is a human being, probably a nice person, and probably someone who works very hard. And he can accomplish your project on a priority basis, he can do it in a half-baked manner, or he can put it at the bottom of his briefcase and make it wait until Monday morning. Yeah, I want to remember his name.

Cy Leslie: Remembering names shows *thoughtfulness.* Thoughtfulness is a very important component to building relationships. And you absolutely can't be thoughtful without memory — that's thought*less*ness.

Take my word for it — we don't really "forget" names. We don't *remember them in the first place,* because we usually don't hear them, or we don't *pay attention* to them, which is next door to not hearing them! (Semantics in platitude form: Something, anything — a name — must be gotten before it can be *for*gotten.)

The idea I'm about to teach you, all my ideas, head inexorably toward one and only one goal, and that is to "trap a fleeting thought," to enable you to, force you to, *get* a name (or any information), *hear* it, *pay attention* to it, be *originally aware* of it, *register* it — remember *it in the first place!*

I started you on this idea when I taught you the first Link some chapters back. One of the things to do (after "airplane" and before "dentist") was to call Jason Carpenter. Without discussion, I simply made "carpenter" part of the list/Link.

You did it without questioning and without my having to go into whys and wherefores — picturing a carpenter (the noun) simply, *automatically,* and unconditionally, told you that you had to call *Mr.* Carpenter! And before that it worked as well when, in the chapter on absentmindedness, I suggested you use "simmer man" to remind you of Mr. Zimmerman. *That* is the basis of my *Substitute Word* System of memory. It will be an important part of the artillery you'll need in your battle against forgetfulness.

It's such a simple concept. You substituted a thought that reminded you of the name. I selected two examples that entailed only an easy, *direct* segue, of course. All I had to do was to use a name that already had *meaning*. There are plenty of those — Wells, Fox, Rockman (rock man), Lyons, Horn, Taylor, Shepherd, Cook, Mailer, Hope, Fine, Hart, Glass, Underwood, Forrest, Coyne, Rivers, Post, Craven, Duncan (dunkin'), Storm. I could fill up pages with examples.

I could also fill up pages with names that have no intrinsic meaning perhaps, but that do conjure up an image in your mind. Any name that's the same as or similar to that of a famous baseball player, for example, will make you think of baseball! DiMaggio, Ruth, Gehrig, Mantle, Mays, Snider. Graham might make you think of *cracker* and Campbell might make you see *soup,* although *camp* and *bell* do also have their own meanings. Lipton would certainly make me think of *tea,* McDonald of a hamburger (or a farm — "Old MacDonald" had one), and Caruso or Sinatra of a singer. Hudson and Jordan would make you think of a river. Easy.

Arlie Lazarus *(President and COO, Jamesway Corporation):* We stress that our people remember other people's names. I think that gives us a competitive advantage over other chains, where they don't know/remember anybody. Knowing a person and remembering, if possible, the spouse's name is *important.* And to this day, when I visit one of my stores, I make sure beforehand to check the names of the people who work there.

Ralph Destino: I know all my store managers' names. It would be desirable to know all the salespeople by name. And we *cannot afford* to forget a client's name. Not when you're dealing with a luxury clientele, the kind we serve. These people expect that when they come into Cartier's they will be appropriately treated — and that they will be remembered. They don't expect this, perhaps, in a department store; here, they expect it. They don't spend $100,000 in Macy's; they do, and more, at Cartier's.

HL: Do you, as chairman, still want to remember names of Cartier clientele?

RD: Oh, yes. Nothing pleases me more than to go down on the floor and greet clients — by name; many by their first names. I love that. And clients — *they* love it. It's important *within* the firm, too. Ken Watson became president of Cartier, Inc., when I moved up to chairman. He's very talented, with all the skills of a modern executive. He has something extra, though — a wonderful way with people who work for us. One of the first things he did was to find out the names of all our people. He attaches a lot of importance to that — and rightfully so.

HL: Would you say, as chairman, that that (among other things, of course) had something to do with his becoming president?

RD: Sure! Sure! I think so.

George J. Konogeris *(Senior Vice President, Kinney Shoe Corporation):* I know most of the names of our store managers — that's a lot of stores, a lot of managers. It's really important for me to remember them; it's a great characteristic. We just promoted a young man from Crystal Lake, Illinois, because customers always asked for him. Why? Well, among other things, he made it his business to remember all of their names, their spouses' and their childrens' names. He'll go far with our company.

Philip A. Bossert: I have to remember all the details of my position, and then there are *people*. I want to remember names (and other facts) of my employees, but also of the people I deal with — printers, producers, designers, agency people, writers — a whole range of people. There's so much to remember because of the complexity of society.

"Complexity of society." It reminds me that many thousands of years ago, when there weren't too many people, only a few within each village, tribe, or clan, it was easy to identify a person. People were named after a characteristic. Mr. Bent Arm *had* a bent arm! Just looking at him *told* you his name. The same for Mr. Hanging Ear, Miss Wide Nostrils, and Mr. Short Leg. American Indians also used descriptive names: Bald Eagle, Running Deer, Big Mouth, Sitting Bull. Later, other names started out as descriptions of a skill or occupation — Hunter, Cooper, *Carpenter*.

But, as populations grew, so did forgetfulness. Because Bent Arm and Wide Nostrils may have had an offspring who had neither a bent arm nor wide nostrils and was called something that meant "son of Bent Arm." It no longer physically described the person. Such names are still used, but it is unlikely that today's Mr. Cooper makes barrels (or that he's even aware of the fact that that's the meaning of the word!).

All right; my system isn't that far away from descriptive, as you'll see when we get to faces. But why not make *any* name meaningful? I mean *now*, not at birth! The two categories I mentioned earlier consist of easy-to-visualize names. But what about a name like Bertrovski. Ordinarily you'd let that go right through your head, in one ear and out the other, if it even *reached* the first ear. Most people simply don't *expect*, therefore don't *attempt*, to remember a name that's more than one syllable.

But break that name down, make it meaningful, and you *can* expect to remember it — and the act of breaking it down, itself, marks your *intention* to remember it! That's important. Ber — *bear*; trov — *trough* (or *tough*); ski — *ski*. Bear trough ski.

That has meaning! It can be visualized. A *bear* sees a *trough* and *ski*s in it! Silly? Sure. But a silly *meaning*, and that's the point. With a bit of that "imaginuity" you can break down, and thereby give meaning to, the most unusual names. Dimitriades — *the meat tree ate E's!* Chesnavich — *chase no witch, chasin' a witch.* Daratsos — *the rat sews.* Stretch that imagination. Theodore — *see a door.* Bartlett — *bottle it* (or see a pear). Aronowitz — *air on a wits* (wits — brains). Fernandez — *fern and S,* or *fern and ass* (donkey). Koscelski — *go sell ski.* Maleszewski (pronounced "mal a chev ski") — *mail a chef (a) ski.* I wanted to remember the name of the head of the mine workers' union in South Africa (as I was reading an article that mentioned him) — Cyril Ramaphosa. I visualized *cereal* and *ram a foe, sir.*

To remember the name Hirabayashi, I thought *here I buy a she!* Make up your own mental picture. I saw an advertisement for a

"Swami Satchidananda," and I overheard someone say, "This guy should change his name to Smith so people can remember it." Well, for most, thinking or seeing "satchel down under" would probably make that name *easier* to remember than Smith.

Unless I told them to visualize a black*smith*'s hammer for Smith. Common names like Smith, Gordon, Cohen, Jones, Brown are easy to lose. Bentavagnia is probably easier to remember (for someone who's trying) because you have to concentrate on it a bit in order to register it at all. Smith and Cohen and Lee seemingly take no concentration or effort, which is why they're easier to lose.

You'll hear them often enough to develop *standard* Substitute Words (or thoughts) for them. I always see a black*smith*'s hammer for Smith (or Smythe or Schmidt — *true* memory tells me the difference), an ice-cream *cone* for Cohen, a *garden* for Gordon, *owns* for Jones, a meadow (*lea*) for Lee. Use these once or twice, and they become standards.

The Substitute Word System: Whenever you *hear* a name, think up a word or phrase that you can visualize and that *sounds enough* like that name to *remind you of it*. Suffixes and prefixes are all that remain for me to discuss. Think of a picture to remind you of each of the common ones, throw that into your association, and you'll have it.

Berg — (ice berg); stein — beer stein; itz — itch; Mc or Mac — Mack truck; witz — wits or witch; ly — lea (meadow); son — son or sun; ger — grr (lion growling) or gar (fish) or ci*gar*; ton — the item is heavy, weighs a ton; baum — bum or bomb; and so on. So, for McKinley, you might see a *Mack* truck *in* a *lea* (Mack in lea). For Greenbaum — a *green bomb*.

Evan R. Bell: I *have* to know a client's wife's or husband's name — children's names. Even *pets'* names!

Richard Schlott: It's important for me to remember names. As president of the company, I try to remember the 125 managers and the top producers among my other 5,000 employees. I want to remember them when I see them at a meeting or function. It shows that I care about them, and makes them care more about me and about the corporation.

HL: Most every top executive I've interviewed feels the same way. And I'm a corporate speaker; I'm at a lot of business functions, and I always see that. I see the top-echelon people remembering the names of the lower-echelon people. I think *all* top management finds that to be very important. They make it a point to use a name, spouse's name, and so on.

RS: I find that to be so with all the corporate heads I know. They care . . .

HL: Do you have to know which manager is at which particular location?

RS: Oh sure. I have to connect a name to say, Greenwich, Connecticut. I also want to remember the secretary's name, and if I knew the intercom number, that'd help too. I do remember the manager's and secretary's names in all my offices.

HL: That's why you're the president, Dick!

RS: I don't know if that's what made me president, but it sure helps!

HL: Can you give me an example where forgetting caused someone to lose points?

Peter Kougasian: I knew a lawyer who crammed most of the night to remember the names of the twelve jurors for the next morning's trial. No faces — she just wanted to use the names as she spoke and looked in the general direction of the jury. She remembered all of them *except one!* That was worse than not remembering any.

It isn't necessary to spend that much time to memorize twelve names. Now that you know how to visualize a name (by thinking up a Substitute Word), you can quickly form a Link with names just as you did with things! Take these names:

Patterson (pat a son)
Gitwelke (get well, key)
Carruthers (car udders)
Bell (bell)

Petrocelli (pet row jelly)
Fleming (flaming)
Tropiano (throw piano)
Smolenski (small lens ski)
Manglanaro (mangle an arrow)
Smith (smith's hammer)
McRae (Mack ray)
Graves (graves)

I've suggested Substitute Words (thoughts or phrases) for twelve jurors' names. Use those or think up your own. Form a Link. You could *start* the Link with (or in) a jury box — that tells you what the Link *pertains to*. Really *see* each picture. There are many ways to go but, as an example: in the jury box, you're *patt*ing *a son* (small look-alike of yourself); your son is giving a *get well* card to a gigantic *key*; a gigantic key is milking a *car* that has *udders* like a cow's; the car with udders is ringing a huge *bell*; your *pet* is *row*ing a bell through *jelly*; your pet (in jelly) is burning, *flaming*; a piano is flaming — you throw it away from you (*throw piano*); a *small* camera (*lens*) is *ski*ing on a piano; a skiing camera crashes into a gigantic arrow and mangles it (*mangle an arrow*); a gigantic arrow is swinging a black*smith*'s hammer (or you're hitting an arrow with the hammer); you're smashing holes in a *Mack* truck with a huge hammer and a bright *ray* shines out of each hole; rays are shining on millions of *graves* (gravestones).

If you've used Substitute Words that will remind you of the names, and if you really tried to *see* each *individual* picture, there's no way you cannot remember them all. If you started your Link in the jury box, that reminds of Patterson. Go from there. Try it.

The methodology applies to names, numbers, *anything*. One of the reasons association works so well is that the very act of forming the picture creates the memory. The same is true for thinking up a Substitute Word (like *car lie L* or *call aisle* for Carlisle), or coming up with a word to represent a number. In all cases, you're forcing (a) interest, (b) observation, (c) attention, (d) concentration, and thus (e) *memory*. And you're using your imagination, a bit of enthusiasm, and curiosity. All those *good* things!

Ruth Mass: It'd be great to remember the name of an established client and the name of the person or corporation he or she recommended to us as a client. That'd be a marvelous aid, part of public relations. I try to see those two people together — to help me remember that one recommended the other. And if I, and my people, could remember the sales rep's name for each airline — what a time-saver that'd be. Those are the people we have to call for information all the time.

Generally speaking, I find that remembering and dropping names in business is very important. So if you can wave that magic wand of yours and give me a great memory in one area, make that area *names!*

Connecting one name to another is no longer a problem; you just did it eleven times. I'll talk about associating a person's name to a company name in the next chapter. Right now, Ruth Mass's problem is easily solved. If Al Hepburn is a longtime client and he recommends Bob Gardner, bind them together with a silly association. You might see a *gardener* working (in a garden) while his *hip burns*. Really see it, and you've got it. By the third or fourth time you've thought of that piece of information, it will be knowledge. *The picture goes but the mind knows.*

And, as you will see, this is only the beginning. The Substitute Word idea will be an invaluable aid to you in many ways.

The merchant said in caustic tones:
"James Henry Charles Augustus Jones,
Please get your pay and leave the store;
I will not need you any more.
Important chores you seem to shun;
You're always leaving work undone;
And when I ask the reason why,
You heave a sad and soulful sigh,
And idly scratch your dome of thought,
And feebly say, 'Oh, I forgot!'
James Henry Charles Augustus Jones,
This world's a poor resort for drones,
For men with heads so badly set
That their long suit is to forget.

No man will ever write his name
Upon the shining wall of fame,
Or soar aloft on glowing wings
Because he can't remember things.
I've noticed that such chaps as you
Remember when your pay is due;
And when the noontime whistles throb,
Your memory is on the job;
And when a holiday's at hand,
Your recollection isn't canned.
The failures on life's busy way,
The paupers, friendless, wan and gray,
Throughout their bootless days, like you,
Forgot the things they ought to do.
So take your coat, and draw your bones,
James Henry Charles Augustus Jones!"

— WALT MASON, *"He Who Forgets"*

13

In Business, It's Who You Know and What You Know about Them

Spouse's Names, Titles, Corporate Affiliations

Not one of the top-level executives I interviewed failed to mention that when it got down to the nitty-gritty, he or she was in a *"people"* business. Of course. Whether you sell a product or a service, you've got to sell it to a *person.* The terminology is, "Send ten gross to Acme Manufacturing Company," but it's Joe Doakes who ordered those ten gross — it's Joe Doakes you had to sell. When I was invited to the Jamesway Corporation headquarters to interview Arlie Lazarus (its president), it happened to be "buyer-seeing" day. The lobby was standing-room-only, just packed with salespeople holding their sample cases, dressed to the nines, nervous — waiting to see the buyer for his or her particular product. You can be sure that each salesperson there wanted to impress the buyer *personally.*

HL: How important is remembering names in your business?

Alan Greenberg: Extremely. Someone calls, he doesn't want a dead fish on this end. I'd like to know who it is, what company he represents. A client wants to know that he's *known,* that he's remembered.

HL: Are you saying that it's possible to upset, even lose, a client if you forget his name?

AG: Yeah! And if you forget his wife's name, you can have real trouble. There's a secret weapon for your book, Harry. Teach how to remember wives' names. It's so important when dealing with important people, because wives are used to being known as Mrs. So-and-so. Take the time to remember wives' names, and you're ahead of the competition.

HL: So it would be important to address her by name and also to ask about her children by name?

AG: She wouldn't forget you if you did. Definitely important, absolutely makes points for you.

Edmond E. Chapus *(President and CEO, Alsthom, Inc. — French engineering/manufacturing firm with 47,000 employees):* It's *very* important for me and those who work for me to remember clients' names, in and out of the office. I don't know if we'd lose a client if we forgot his or her name, but it's sure a plus when we remember the client's name *and* the spouse's name as well.

Vincent Sardi *(Sardi's restaurant, New York City):* Oscar Hammerstein and his wife used to eat here quite often. One afternoon, Mrs. Hammerstein came in with a friend. I was at the door in those days, and I recognized her. I said, "Good afternoon, Mrs. Hammer*steen.*" She stopped, looked at me coldly, and said, "The name is Hammer*stein,* and don't you ever forget it!" Well, that was awfully embarrassing and I sure didn't want it to happen again. Of course, the thing that came to mind was a beer stein. That solved the problem. To this day, when I think of Hammerstein, I think of a beer stein. It's very important to get names *right.*

First names are handled just like last names. Make them meaningful. After a while, you'll have a standard Substitute Word for just about every given name, because you'll hear (or meet) them often.

For Betty, bet E; Harry, hairy; Jim, gym; Seymour, see more; Bill, (dollar) bill; Robert, robber; Morton, more ton; Douglas, dug glass or dug less; Walter, wall tear; Samuel, 's a mule or (just) mule; Wallace, wall lace; Norman, no man; Prescott, press cot; Dexter, deck stir or decks tar; Gerard, chair hard; Barney, bar knee; Sandra, sand draw; Renée, grenade or run hay; Esther, ess (S) tear or yes dear; Mary, marry (see a wedding); Eileen, I lean or eye lean; Beatrice, beat rice or bead dress; Abigail, a big ale; Alvira, I'll wire her; Jacob, shake up; Percy, purse see; Daphne, deaf knee; and on and on.

These are but a few suggestions for Substitute Words for given names. They're easy to make up; usually the first thing that comes to mind is best. When I needed a Substitute Word for Ralph, I thought of *rough*. I've been using that for forty years!

Associating a spouse's first name to the "important person's" name should be a cinch for you now. Mr. Hayes's wife is Judith. Associate *hay* (or *A's*) to *chewed it*. Mrs. Ryan's first name is Kathleen. A *cat* is *lean* because it keeps eating b*rine*. Mrs. Hall's husband is Mark. See gigantic *marks* all over a *hall*. These are suggestions only; make up your own Substitute Words and pictures.

The best way to assure yourself that this works perfectly is to *do* it the next time you want to remember a spouse's first name. Right now, assure yourself by turning to chapter 4 and taking Test 2 again. Please *don't* continue reading until you've done so.

Handle the name of a corporation exactly as you would the name of a person. So — if the sales rep for Delta Airlines is Ms. Corrigan, get *dealt* and *car again* into one silly picture (I was *dealt a car again*). If you want to remember Ms. Corrigan's first name — Lucy — get a *loose E* (or lose E) into that picture. American Airlines — Mr. Wright; see yourself *writ*ing on an American flag. Pan Am — Ms. Nugent; a *new gent* (see a shiny gentleman) is cooking in a large *pan*. United — Bill Warren; *bill*s are *warring,* then they get together, they *unite*. Eastern — Miranda Beck; see *E's turn*ing on a *veranda* and *peck*ing each other.

HL: Are affiliations — who is with which company — important for you to remember?

Michael K. Stanton: It's *imperative* to remember that. Certainly in the business arena, but also in a social situation.

HL: So remembering names and faces and affiliations is as important to a corporate lawyer as it is in any business?

MKS: Of course. It's possible to lose clients if you don't show them the courtesy of remembering.

HL: In your position, is remembering affiliations important to you?

Frank V. AtLee: Oh, yes. If you have a mission to accomplish. I want to, and I want my people to, remember which company someone is with. And not only his title, but exactly what his function is within that company. You know, there are chief chemists and there are *chief* chemists; there are purchasing agents and there are buyers, so it's not only the title, it's what that person really does in that responsibility.

I've shown you how to remember corporate affiliations. And as Frank AtLee mentioned, you might also want to be reminded of a person's position within a corporation. Make up a picture to represent every possible title and use them as needed. To give you the idea, first using what are not necessarily business titles: For "doctor," get a *stethoscope* into your association (a hypodermic needle or thermometer would work as well; I've *always* used "stethoscope" to force me to remember the title "doctor"). For a lieutenant — *tenant;* captain — *cap;* major — *amaze ya';* general — picture *stars.* It's easy, and fun, to make them up.

To remind you of chairman, picture a *chair,* of course. For president, a *press* or *press*ing clothing. For vice president, all you'd need is *vise* or *V ice.* Director of sales — *wreck tore* would do it, but it's as easy to visualize someone directing something — in this case, directing sailboats, sails.

So, if you want to remember that Mr. Compari is with Xerox (I'm making up the names), you can see someone *sear*ing *E's* on *rocks* and *compar*ing them — *sear rocks, compare E.* He may be director of marketing. You can see the above action happening in a *market;* you're *direct*ing it. Mr. Bennett is president of Raffman and Company. See a *man* on a *raft bend*ing a gigantic *net,* then *press*ing it. *Bend net, raft man; press* — president. (Please bear in mind, and this warrants repetition, these need be only instant, but *clear,* pictures in your mind — really *one* picture. It takes me *much* longer to explain it than it does for you to see it.) Mr. Lawrence Kuszak is chairman of Home Insurance Company. *Cues* in a *sack* destroying a *home,* which is covered by *insurance.* If you want to get the first name and position into the picture, *lower ants* and *chair* will do it.

Once you're familiar with the concept, it gets easier and easier. For vice president of sales, you might always use *vise sails* or a *vise* making *sales;* for comptroller — controller or count roller; for treasurer — treasure; marketing and research — searching in a market. And, one more point: You can include your "position reminder" in the original picture, or you can just associate the person's name to the corporation. Then, after you have that, form a separate picture connecting the person's name to his or her position. Either way is fine. For example, say you've made an association to help you remember that Mr. Kuszak is with Home Insurance Company. You know that. Then you form a separate association of *cue sack* to *chair,* to tell you that he's the chairman. Try both ways.

I think you've got it now. Try it. Turn to page 30 and take Test 6 again — before you go any further.

Some executives told me that if they learned *nothing else* but simply how to *know* who belongs with which corporation and exactly what that person's position is, they'd be thrilled. Well, if you've done as I've suggested and have taken Test 6 again, you *know* how easy it is, how well the technique works. Tests are fine, but actually applying the technique in your business is a thousand times better. And this is only a scratch on the scratch of the surface of what you're capable of accomplishing!

Vincent Sardi *(Sardi's restaurant, New York City):* Is memory necessary in the restaurant business? Definitely. It's just about essential.

One important thing for a restaurant host to remember is not only who goes with whom, but never to get personal. A man may not be with his wife, or vice versa. The best thing is not to get personal *at all.* One example: Oscar Levant, the pianist and actor, came into the restaurant. I said, "Mr. Levant, you certainly lost a lot of weight. . . . You look really trim." I didn't know he was a dedicated hypochondriac. He shouted, "What do you mean? That I'm sick!" And he walked out — and never, never came back. (Well, he came back only if he couldn't avoid it, an opening-night party, or something like that.) I learned a lesson. I certainly should have *remembered* not to do that, not to get personal.

14

Learning and Retrieving Business-related Codes and Letters

Stock Symbols, Style Numbers, Computer Codes, Business Spelling, and More

If you want to, have to, remember style numbers consisting of letters or of letters and numbers, or stock market symbols, or anything that consists of or contains letters, you'll need to have a way to *visualize* letters — which, after all, are really nothing more than squiggles with a sound attached.

The idea I've devised is consistent with the ideas and techniques you've been using up to now. I showed you how to make a name (a conglomeration of sounds) meaningful by applying the Substitute Word System, and you can visualize numbers thanks to the Peg System (Phonetic Number/Alphabet). The same basic idea works for letters; they have to be turned into tangible, visual entities.

Use a word that *sounds like* the letter, or *reminds* you of it for any other reason. It doesn't stretch the imagination too much to decide that the word (or picture of a) *dean* (of a college) should represent the letter **d**. Or that an *eye* will represent the letter **i**, or that *hen* can represent (*remind* you of) the letter **n**.

Go over the following list once, perhaps twice, and you'll have another weapon to use in your war against *forgetting*. I'm listing more than one letter word for most of the letters. Make your choice, then use that one all the time (although there's no rule that says you can't use more than one).

A – ape, hay

B – bean, beat

C – sea, see (binoculars)

D – dean, deal (cards)

E – eel, eek (scream)

F – half, **eff**ervescent

G – jeans, gee

H – ache, age, itch

I – eye, I

J – jail, jaybird

K – cake, cane, key

L – el(evated) train, hell

M – hem, ham, **em**peror

N – hen, **en**trance, **en**ema

O – eau (water), owe, h**ole**

P – pea, peek

Q – cue, queue

R – hour (clock), **ar**gue, **aar**dvark

S – ess curve, ass, **esc**ape

T – tea, tee, T-square

U – ewe, **eu**nuch, **u**niverse

V – veal, V (victory sign)

W – Waterloo, trouble you

X – X-ray, eggs

Y – wine, wild

Z – zebra

The first word listed for each is the one I usually use. For B, I use ''bean'' — not ''bee'' — so as not to confuse it with the Peg Word for 9.

That's all you'll ever need for remembering letters — that, or a word that begins and ends with two vital letters. For instance, if the style number of, say, a lamp, is BD, see a gigantic lamp sleeping in **bed**; or you pull the chain on a bed and it lights up — it's a lamp. The word "bed" will *remind* you of BD because *you* thought of it. (Bean/dean would do the same.)

This idea can be used in conjunction with the Phonetic Number/ Alphabet, if a style number consists of letters and a number. Perhaps the style number of the lamp is BD1. Well, you can form any of a variety of associations. "Bedde**d**" would do it — you'd *know* that the last sound represents 1. Or, "**bad** *tie*"; see a lamp spanking a bad (awful) tie. If the style number is BD47, you can think of "**bed** *rock*." When you actually put this idea to work, you'll see that your *true* memory will tell you that "bed rock" is BD47 not 91RK! That's because *you* will be thinking up the word or phrase *yourself* to solve *your* specific problem.

If the style number consists of three (or more) letters, make up a longer reminder word or phrase and associate it to the item. "**Leper**" could be your reminder word for LPR. (No, you wouldn't think that "leper" represented 594 [although it could], because you'd *know* that you're dealing with letters.)

But you can always also use the individual letter words. For BD, you could see a gigantic *bean* wearing a mortarboard (what I always see for dean) — it's the *dean*. If you want to get lamp in there, see millions of beans flying out of the lamp when you light it — and the lamp is wearing a mortarboard. For MJ, you might visualize a dress (what I see for *hem*) — just the dress, no woman in it — in *jail*. A *cue* (stick) being *X-ra*yed reminds of QX.

So, there are different ways to go to remember letters. Just being aware of the options will enable you to fall into the way that works best for you, for your circumstances, automatically. Or try different ways at first, then use what works best.

Right now, if you're familiar with the letter words, flip back to chapter 4, take Test 10 again, and surprise yourself. You deserve a pat on the back for the progress *you'll see* you've made!

HL: Harvey, you showed me a tracking sheet that listed radio station call letters in every major city. Do you have to remember those letters? And the city?

Harvey Leeds: I sure do. Of course, I can look them up on that sheet, but I'd save a week of man hours every year if I *knew* them. Not only that, I'd impress the heck out of my peers and superiors. (I *do* impress the heck out of them — thanks to you, Harry.)

Use the Substitute Word System to visualize, and remind you of, a city name, and the letter word idea to do the same for letters, and Harvey Leeds's chore of recalling radio station call letters becomes much easier to handle.

Just about all the call letters for radio stations in America start with W or K. Usually, the stations in one city will *all* start with the same letter. All the stations in the Los Angeles area start with K. That becomes a known after a while. (If not, the letter word for K goes into the picture.)

In Long Beach, the call letters are KNAC. Do you see how easily that information can be locked in? How you can force one fact to remind you of the other? See a gigantic *hen* (N) and a large *ape* (A) running along the *sea* (C) on a *long beach*. If you needed the K, you'd put a cake or cane into the picture. In Boston, there's WBCN; *boss* (or Boston *beans*) and **bacon** did it for me! But you could also associate *boss* (and *ton*, if you think you need it) to *bean, see, hen*.

J. K. Hartman: It isn't necessary to remember stock symbols today, but it sure is faster and saves lots of time if you do. You have to punch the symbol letters into the computer in order to get the current price. Punch it in without looking for the book in order to look up the symbol and you eliminate a middleman. It's a time-management advantage.

You can now *visualize* the letters of stock symbols. If you see them along with the *company name,* they're easy to remember. The symbol for Boeing is BA. You can see someone *bowing* (Boeing) while *beans* (B) are being thrown at him by an *ape* (A). Or you could see someone bowing as he receives his B.A. degree.

The symbol for Marion Labs is MKC. A large dress (*hem*/M) is *marryin'* in a *lab*oratory. It holds up a wedding *cake* (K) for all to *see* (C). Polaroid is PRD; you approach and **prod** a camera, or a *polar* bear. Or, associate *pea, hour, dean* to camera or polar bear. (A million peas fly out of a clock and hit a dean, who's taking a picture of it with his camera.) Schlumberger Limited (French pronunciation, "shlum ber zhay") is SLB. You can see a **slob** *slumber*ing; or you're slumbering on an *ess curve* (S) of an **el**evated train (L) covered with *beans* (B). Chrysler Corporation is C. See a Chrysler car or Manhattan's Chrysler Building in the *sea* (C). (You *could* also see someone *cry* in cole *slaw* — cry enough to make a sea.) Newmont Mining: NEM. Visualize a shiny *new mount*ain; there's a *hen* (N) and an *eel* (E) eating a *hem* or a *ham* (M) on top.

Control Data Company: CDA. A lion tamer is *control*ing *dates* instead of lions; he's doing it in the *sea,* wearing a *dean*'s hat — the dean is an *ape.* Philip Morris, Inc.: MO. *Moe* is the diminutive of Morris. Or your *ma is* (Morris) throwing her dress (*hem*/M) into *eau* (water/O). Borden, Inc.: BN. You *bought* a *den* full of *beans* and *hens.* (Or associate bought den to **bin**.)

I've used many words to suggest simple, instant mind pictures. Of course, if you can picture something that reminds you of a company (a substitute thought) instead of breaking it down (Substitute Word or phrase), do so. Picturing a *bottle of milk* would make me think of Borden. A **ban** on milk would really give me the information I need. It's important to me, and to you, to realize that even if this idea doesn't work, it *has to work!* You're forcing yourself to pinpoint your attention and concentration — without pain. You *must* remember better than you ever did before!

Some may not think that spelling correctly is important in business. Some do. Mark H. McCormack, in his book *What They Don't Teach You at Harvard Business School* (Bantam Books, 1984), wrote that he insists that any communication over his name "is neatly typed and contains no spelling errors."

Would you have confidence in my teaching if misspelled words were sprinkled throughout this book? I don't think so, and I wouldn't blame you. When I receive two résumés for one position, I don't bother interviewing the person who sent the one containing misspellings, even though he or she may be better suited for that particular position — I'd never know it. All the executive-level people I spoke to feel the same way: *You can't sell it if you can't spell it!*

I can give you some help with a typical spelling problem or two — because they are also *memory* problems. One touchy area: Is a word spelled with an **e** or an **a?** Knowing the letter words can help answer that question. For example, the common error in spelling the word "separate" is using an **e** instead of an **a** ("seperate"). You'll always remember to use an **a** if you visualize yourself "separating" an *ape* — you're splitting an ape in half. (Or an ape is separating something.) Ape *tells* you that it's an **a** near the center of that word. Similarly, you can see a gigantic *eel* going up in an "elevator"; an *ape* selling "insurance"; an *eel* being born, coming into "existence." See yourself pouring *tea* on a "mortgage." See an *eel* writing on "stationery" and an *ape* remaining "stationary."

Another way to avoid common spelling errors is to force one simple word to remind you of the correct spelling *within* a word that's more difficult to spell. My favorite example (I've used it since a teacher of mine taught it in second grade): Never be**lie**ve a *lie*. Think of that and you'll never misspell the word "believe" again. The same idea works for other tricky words: To "inter**rupt**" is to *err;* a "**ball**oon" is shaped like a *ball;* tell a *secret* to your "**secret**ary," *all* lines are "par**all**el," there's *iron* in our "env**iron**ment," you *miss* out when you "**miss**pell," and so forth.

All right! (*Not* "alright.")

Bernadette Skubly-Butts: It's important for me to remember what's in our computers, but more important to remember the *computer formats* — what codes to punch in to get the information I need. For example, I may have to know how many seats are left in all sections of a particular flight. I'd have to remember the code letters FG; then I punch in FG, the flight number and date — and all the vital information would immediately come up on the screen. There are over twenty of these codes; each brings up different information. Information like important holidays in France, when the Grand Prix happens, different meal services, delayed flights, et cetera. It would be of some great help and save me *much* time if I could remember/know all those codes.

Companies *know* that this type of memory problem exists. Those that come to me, or use my systems, solve the problem. Others . . . well, Bernadette Skubly-Butts showed me a pamphlet that Air France sends to all its offices, about "Francis," the airline's computer system. The booklet is called *Aide Memoire* — "aid to memory." The problem is, as Bernadette said, "Actually, all it is is a list of the codes and the information to expect when we punch in that code, or format. It doesn't tell us *how* to remember them."

Now that you know how to visualize letters, make them tangible, this problem is easily solved. FG: think of **fig**, or *half* (F) a pair of *jeans* (G) and associate it to "available seats." Do it any way you like. If *you* thought of, and visualized, *figs* sitting in all *available seats,* or *half jeans* sitting in all available seats, you've got it. By the third or fourth time you punch in FG, you won't have to think of your silly picture anymore — it will be *knowledge. That's* an *aide memoire!*

Many of the simple computer codes begin with the letter W. One is WR, for "search." Now, if you already *know* that all these codes start with W, all you need to remember is R. Visualize yourself *searching* for a clock (*hour*/R). If you want the *two* letters, either *searching* for someone during a **war**, or Napoleon (I picture him for Waterloo!) searching for a clock would do. That's all.

WI is the format code for "print." See words being *print*ed on your *eye,* or on Napoleon's eye. WL means "retrieve list." A very long *list* is on an *el*evated train, or you drop an important list down a **well**, or list things on a **wall**. There are many ways to go; the one *you* decide on is usually best for you. (You realize, of course, that if the computer codes were *numbers,* exactly the same approach would apply — since you can use the Peg System to make numbers tangible and visual.)

There's one format in the airline's computer that has to do with groups, or, more specifically, "cancellation of groups." Once you're in that format, a single letter codes the reason for cancellation. Example: the letter D means "could not confirm space." See a *dean* (D) trying to get space, but no one will confirm it for him. *See* it and you'll *remember* it. N means "insufficient number of participants." A *hen* (N) is lonely, or can't get enough participants to lay eggs! I don't care how silly you get — *you* thought of it; it'll work. F stands for "competition offered a better fare." *Half* (F) fare. (You might see *half* a county *fair*.) Easy, isn't it?

It's also important for airline people and travel agents to know the three-letter codes for airports in different cities. Yes, they can be looked up, but when you want to punch an airport code into your computer, it's *so* much faster simply to know it. That's what *every* travel agent and airline employee tells me.

As a traveler, I like to know these codes also. I want to see MSY on my baggage claim check and *know* that my luggage is being checked through to *New Orleans*. In many, or most, cases the letters are an abbreviation of the airport name or city, like ATL for Atlanta, or BOS for Boston. Those are easy. MSY for New Orleans can be a problem. But not if you associate *oar leans* to **Missy**, or to *hem* (M), *ess* (S) curve, *wine* (Y). (If you wanted to remember that it's *Logan* Airport in Boston, just associate "hel**lo again**" or *"low can"* to Boston beans.)

FCO is Fiumicino Airport in Rome, Italy. Associate *few* or *"fume, gee no"* to *roam* in order to know that — remember that — name and location. *"Half sea owe"* to Rome does it for the airport code. Visualize half the sea going to Rome (or roaming) because it owes itself that trip. An *oar landing* on an MC (master of ceremonies) who shouts, "Oh!" tells you that MCO means the Orlando (McCoy) airport. (An oar lands and says, "Me coy.")

I would like to give you every example I can think of where this idea of making letters meaningful would apply. There simply isn't enough space for that. But now that you know the technique (and the letter words), there's no reason for you ever again *not* to be able to remember letters of the alphabet and whatever it is that's connected to them.

Joseph V. Casale *(President, Active Concern, Inc., representing Phoenix Insurance Companies):* I went to Jesuit school, and Jesuits believe in memory. We had to memorize all the soliloquies of Hamlet, the Greek alphabet, et cetera. They believed in that as mind training, which, of course, it is — exercising the muscles of your mind. No, I don't use notes when I speak to an audience. The Jesuits insisted that you not read; you had to speak from knowledge, from *memory.* I hate the idea of someone reading his speech to me.

Arlie Lazarus *(President and COO, Jamesway Corporation):* I speak to audiences two or three times a week. I list key words; a key word for each point I want to make.

HL: Would it be important to you if I taught you to *know* definitely all the points you want to cover?

AL: Oh, without a doubt, extremely important and helpful. You mean I wouldn't need that index card? Great!

15

Remember Speeches and Sales Reports Easily and Confidently

Read or Listen and Remember Any Business Material

Did you know that the number-one universal fear is not death? Death is number three or number four on the list. The number-one fear is facing and speaking to an audience! The reason for that universal fear? In most cases, it's *fear of forgetting* what you want to say and looking like a fool. This is obviously not so among corporate executives, since most of them do speak in front of audiences quite often. I asked those I interviewed if they used notes to help them deliver their speeches.

Ralph Destino: Never. If I speak on a new subject, perhaps I'd list key thoughts. I speak about things I know. And when I'm in the audience and the speaker reads or continually looks at notes, I may not turn him off completely, but I am disappointed, and my attention span will surely be shortened.

Michael K. Stanton: Rarely. If you go through the steps of preparing an outline of your speech or a summary of your points, you'll no longer need the written notes. Most often, you're going to do it better and more effectively if you just go do it — no notes.

I sometimes tell a story about a speaker who walks to the lectern after being introduced and reaches into his pocket for his voluminous notes. They're not there! He searches through all his pockets — no notes. Nervous and upset, he stammers his opening line: "Wh-when I arrived this eve-evening only G-God and I kn-new what I was g-going to s-s-say. Now only G-God knows!''

Evan R. Bell told me: "Yes, I use notes, but only an index card with key thoughts. I wouldn't want to be like the guy in that anecdote. It'd be of immeasurable help if I could be as sure of my memory as I am of the written notes.''

A. S. Clausi: I handle speeches three ways. The best is when I do it extemporaneously — with a lot of previous planning. Next best is one-word or one-thought notes. Reading the speech is third, and worst. The main problem is — as you point out — not to forget a point you want to make.

Alan Greenberg: I don't use notes during a business or charity talk. I usually know the subject pretty well, and I just use your Link System of memory to remember the sequence of thoughts and facts. Even though I know the subject well, I don't want to leave out an important point.

Good speakers don't allow themselves to be locked into using notes. Begin with the assumption that the speaker knows the information, knows what he wants to say. What's needed is a way to *remember the thoughts in sequence* so that no key point is forgotten — the problem A. S. Clausi and Alan Greenberg touch on above. You already have a way: the Link system! Look back right now to chapter

7. The items in the Link I taught you there (book, radio, accountant, airplane . . .) could just as well have been the *key words* in a speech, those that would remind you of the complete thoughts.

The key word here is *key word!* There is no thought that can be written or verbalized (or both) from which you cannot extract one word or phrase that will *bring that thought to mind.* Knowing that and knowing how to form a Link is the basis of this method. Just Link the key words of your speech or sales report. And because you know how to make up words to represent numbers, and how to use a Substitute Word to remind you of a name, that information can be included in your Link.

What a simple idea! You've written the speech (or had it written for you), and you highlight or underline the words *you* know will bring the thoughts to mind. Then, *mentally* highlight or underline them by Linking them.

> **Edmond E. Chapus:** I try not to use notes, because I think the delivery is more natural and you get the attention of the people much more when you look at them and speak [seemingly] extemporaneously. You can sense the mood of your audience much better if you do not look down at notes.

Say you want to speak about your corporation's store locations (real estate), sales, computer system, new product line, personnel training, shipping, and advertising. The following Link would do it: *Stores* are *sail*ing on water; gigantic *computers* are sailing; there's a *line* of sparkling (*new*) computers; many people (*personnel*) are standing in a line; you're packing personnel into corrugated cartons to *ship* them; gigantic shipping cartons have billboards, *advertisements,* on them.

This Link of seven key words could help you remember a ten- to fifteen-minute talk or a one-hour speech — according to how much you have to say about each point and how much time you want to take saying it. (All executives know that the biggest mistake in delivering a speech is wandering off the point or going on too long — or both. There are catchphrases to remind you *not* to do that, like: KISS — keep it simple [or short], stupid; the three S's — stand up, speak up, shut up; and tell 'em what you're going to tell 'em, tell 'em, tell 'em what you've told 'em.)

I asked Casey Fleming (not his real name; he prefers anonymity), CEO of his company and a student of mine, to give me an example of a sales report. A cut-down version follows. I've changed the product names, and numbers, but the report remains pretty true to the original. And I've inserted, in brackets, what Casey and I might visualize and Link. Read it over, then form the Link, and you'll have *memorized* the report.

As you know, our four new-model typewriters, those we're calling the Four Aces [*four typewriters* playing cards, one holds the *four aces*] have been on the market for a year now. Two are doing quite well. The portable model number 46 [you're *carrying* a gigantic *roach*] surprised us. It has grossed $2,625,000. [Roach to **new channel** (the speaker *knows* that he's dealing with single-digit millions.)] The electronic model number 47 also did well: it grossed $3,500,000. [*Rock* — **my laces**; get *electricity* — for "electronic" — in there, if you feel you'd need it.]

It's the two "intelligent" models, number 48 and number 49, the memory-capable machines, that are problematic. [On a *roof* is a gigantic *rope*; the rope is *intelligent* but has a *problem* — it can't remember, no *memory*. See it searching for things as if it has *forgotten* where they are.] Model number 49, the 16K machine [that's 16K of memory — rope/*dish cake*] just barely held its own; it grossed $400,000 [**roses**; you can see yourself *barely holding* on to them]. The big disappointment is model number 48, the 8K machine [*roof* to ivy *cake,* or *fake*]; it lost money. [Perhaps you tasted the cake made of ivy and it's a *disappointment* — then it gets *lost.*]

One major headache has been Hudson Data Company, our chip supplier. [So many *dates* and *chips* are floating down the *Hudson* River that you get a major headache.] Shipments are always late and the S14 [**stair**] chips were sent a number of times instead of the R14's [**radar**]. We're looking for a new chip manufacturer.

The Pathé Advertising Company [*path, path A, passé, paté*]

came up with the Four Aces idea and started the promotion campaign, but there, too, we may make a change. [Make change of a dollar.] We may move the account to Brand, Clark Associates. [*Brand* a *clock*].

All these things are now open to discussion. Let's hear some of your thoughts.

It's an individual thing; some would Link just the words, phrases, or thoughts suggested; others wouldn't need all of them; and some would include more pictures to remind them of more details.

On April 13, 1987, Chairman **Arthur Levitt, Jr.,** delivered a speech at the annual meeting of the American Stock Exchange. The opening of his talk was a reminder of the good news he had reported at the previous annual meeting. Then he went on to show that 1986 had been an even better year than 1985, and quoted the following statistics:

In 1986, our equity volume climbed 41.7 percent.

Our options volume rose 34.6 percent.

Our revenues were up 21.0 percent.

And new listings, up 39.1 percent, topped the 100 mark for the first time in 14 years.

The speech went on for a few more pages, of course, but it's the kind of information cited above that I want to discuss. Try this: Visualize yourself throwing away your tea — *quit tea* (equity); it makes such a loud noise (*volume*) that it gives you a hea**rtach**e (41.7).

A *cop chins* (options) until he gets a heartache (you want each piece of information to lead to the next); he sees a rose making lots of noise (*volume rose*) as it joins in a **march** (34.6).

As you're marching, you *rev news* (instead of an engine — revenues; just news or money would do also); the news floats *up,* you catch it in a *net* (21).

An enormous net *lists* (leans — or it's full of written lists) as it's **mopped** (39.1) up. You're mopping up a spinning *top* with the *mark* of a **disease** (100) on it; the mark is shaped like a **tire** (14 years).

I've included many words or pictures here that I'd ordinarily not bother with because I'd already *know* that information. I'm using them only as teaching examples. As you work with this idea on your own speeches, you will see how simple it is and how few words you'll probably need as reminders.

> **HL:** If I could give you a great memory in one area, which area would you choose?
> **Peter Kougasian:** I'd love to be able to remember informational reading material. What a boon that'd be. The last thing I do every night is read the *New York Law Journal* — it's a daily paper — and I try to remember the criminal cases recorded there. Remembering what I read would help me in law tremendously. It would also help me in life.

I will use some specific "law-reading" examples in chapter 25. But in *all* careers, we ingest most of our information via reading and listening. The techniques I've been discussing here apply not only to delivering a speech or sales report but also to remembering a speech or sales report you *hear*. There's no better way to *"force-focus"* your attention and concentration as you listen.

Every how-to-listen-effectively course boils down to two words: *pay attention.* But not one of these courses tells you *how* to do that. The problem, you see, is that most people *think* four times faster than the other person *speaks*. So, there's too much time available for *mind wandering.* How, then, can you keep your mind from wandering, which is the same as *not* paying attention?

Well, one way is to ask questions of the speaker mentally, or to ask them of yourself *about* the speaker: "Oh yeah? Are you going to prove that?" Or, "I wonder how he's going to prove that?" The point is that by asking questions, you keep your mind *there,* on the subject — and you cut down on "wandering" time. That's all right; it does help.

But the *best* way is to Link the points the speaker is making *as* he's making them. You have the time to do so — that four-to-one discrepancy between the speed of your thinking and his speaking (plus the extra time you'll have during anecdotes, asides, and "hems and haws"). Of course, after applying the idea for a while, you'll be Linking the points you want to remember faster and faster. You may even have to include (Link) some minor points, just to keep your attention *pinpointed,* to keep your mind from wandering. The idea works beautifully when listening to a speech, or during a meeting, when a sales report is being presented — because that's the *point* of my systems! They *force* attention and concentration. Mind wandering is *out* while forming a Link! The same techniques apply to remembering reading material.

The following item is paraphrased from a September 1987 business article. It might very well be a report you *hear*. For teaching purposes, however, let's assume you're reading it.

> Malrite Communications Group Inc. announced that it has completed the sale of KMVP-AM and KRXY-FM, its Denver radio stations, to Capital Cities/ABC for 10.7 million. The company will report a gain on this transaction in the third quarter. Proceeds from the sale will go toward reducing long-term debt. Malrite Communications operates 11 radio and 6 television stations.

To remember it, you might link the following: *mail right* (arm) to *communicating* with a *group* (via an announcement) to *sail move up* (or *hem veal pea*) I *am* (AM) to *clock* (hour/R) *eggs wine* (or **Roxy**) **fume** (FM) to *den-radio* to *capital* domes reciting the ABCs to **task** (10.7) to *gain ma* (gain in third quarter) to *reduce* to *owing money* (debt) to **tide** (11)-*radio* to **sh**oe (6)-*television*. (Please bear in mind that if you are interested in the information, if it's part of *your* business, it all becomes clearer and easier. Also, you wouldn't need all the associations. In this example, you probably wouldn't have needed "communicating, group," for instance. *Try* the idea with some of your business material — and see.)

In the chapters to come, there are more examples of this technique and how it can be applied to legal, medical, and similar complex material. It's that important; I want you to understand and *use* these ideas for giving speeches, listening to reports, and digesting reading materials more effectively.

HL: You're one of the funniest people I know. In order to be a comic, do you have to have a good memory?

Charles Nelson Reilly *(Actor, Director):* Oh sure; you have to remember a lot — you have to be a filing cabinet. You have to remember jokes that fit all different situations. If someone mentions "animals," I immediately see animal jokes in my mind; if he mentions "doctor," I see numerous doctor jokes. What is that if not memory?

HL: As a director, how often would you put up with the excuse "I forgot" from your actors?

CNR: That never happens. Nobody says that to me. Theater actors know that's part of the job; you don't say to a director, "I forgot."

16

"Staying/Graying" Power

Double *the Memory Power You Had at Twenty!*

I n his seventies, President Ronald Reagan was probably the most popular, most well known, man in the world, and, he had *power*. What's interesting to me, and should be to you, is that his popularity and his power started to wane when (in 1987) he started to *forget* things. For months, comedians did jokes about his forgetfulness. I, myself, was asked to be part of a pilot television show (NBC-TV), on which I would explain (in a humorous fashion) how he could have remembered the date on which he signed the okay for sending arms to Nicaragua — and so on. The point is, when executives *forget*, people lose confidence in them, which leads to losing power.

Arlie Lazarus, President and COO of the Jamesway Corporation, is a hands-on executive, closely involved with the day-to-day running of his business. Jamesway Corporation operates over 100 miniature "department" stores.

AL: I've been president of Jamesway for over ten years. I sometimes say to my wife, "When do you lose it? Will I ever slow down? What will happen if I lose my memory?" I've thought about it — if I lose my ability to remember — my God, you're really nothing without your memory. It's the first thing I thought of when I had a concussion some years ago. I wish you'd discuss that in your book — older people, retired people, the slow-down process.

HL: Actually, Arlie, I believe that one reason, maybe the main reason, for the general inefficiency I see today is that men or women who reach, say, age sixty-five — and have been doing their work for perhaps forty years — are now forced to retire. These people *know* what they are doing. Now their shoes are filled — poorly — by young people with little or no experience. (Experience *is* memory, isn't it — remembering past events in your area of expertise?) Inefficiency rears its unknowing head. And I've proved that a person at seventy, seventy-five, or more, can have a *better* memory than at age forty! All that's necessary is to *use* — stimulate — your memory properly.

AL: I do see that in my own organization. People get older and don't lose a thing. It's my experience that older people tend to be better as store managers, for example.

Mel Brooks agrees: "In many cases, give me one seventy- or seventy-five-year-old with *experience* over three or four new young people." I can assure Arlie Lazarus that so long as he keeps his mind active — and one great way to do this is to use my systems, which he does — he doesn't have to worry about "losing it" (barring accidents and disease, of course). That's been a cry of mine for almost forty years. But I gotta be honest — George Clemenceau said it long before: "I have discovered the fountain of youth. The secret is simple. Never let your brain grow inactive and you will keep young forever."

And now, it seems, scientists — neurobiologists, neuroscientists, physiologists, endocrinologists — are catching up. As long ago as 1911, a pioneering neurobiologist, Santiago Ramón y Cajal, suggested that "cerebral exercise" could benefit the brain (mind).

But for years, when I said that people who apply my memory systems do not lose brain cells as they age (as we've been led to believe most people do), but may even *gain* brain cells, the scientists pooh-poohed me. Well, now their own research shows "that development and growth of the brain go on into old age." A team of researchers led by Dr. Marian Diamond, Professor of Physiology at the University of California at Berkeley, came to that conclusion, as detailed in an article by Daniel Goleman in the *New York Times* (June 30, 1985). The researchers admitted according to the article, that "it was once thought that the brain was fixed by late childhood, according to innate genetic design." But no longer. So, simply applying the systems taught in this book offers you the best of both worlds — you'll be exercising your mind *and* getting ahead in business!

The *Times* article cites a report in *Experimental Neurology,* by the same researchers that says that "even in old age the cells of the cerebral cortex respond to an enriched environment by forging new connections to other cells." Within the context, "enriched environment" meant a *stimulating* environment, one in which the mind had to be more active. For rats, a bare, small cage with a single occupant was an impoverished environment. A roomier cage where many rats wandered through mazes, ran on wheels, and climbed ladders was an enriched environment. *Old* rats in a stimulating environment showed increased thickening of the cortex — which was a sign that brain cells *increased in size and activity.* The glial cells (of which Albert Einstein had an unusually large number) multiplied and the tips of the brain cells' dendrites lengthened.

Dr. Diamond's research suggests that nerve cells grow no matter what one's age in response to intellectual enrichment (read "exercise" or *use* — using your *imagination* and memory) of all kinds, even crossword puzzles — "anything that stimulates the brain with novelty and challenge." It was found that the dendritic projections act like muscles. Dr. Arnold Scheibel, Professor of Psychiatry at the University of California at Los Angeles, says that "they grow more the more they're used." You can set off dendritic "fireworks" by learning a new language, or trying to learn one, when you're older.

And in his book *Aging Myths* (McGraw-Hill), Dr. Siegfried Kra, Cardiologist and Associate Clinical Professor of Medicine at the Yale

University School of Medicine, writes that "confusion . . . and memory loss are not part of the aging process." He goes on to say that the majority of people (80 percent) who live to old age are *not* troubled by "memory impairment."

In my opinion, people who use my systems tend to hold back senility! Same reasoning: the "muscle" is being exercised. According to the *New York Daily News* (April 30, 1987), today's research, including that of the National Institutes of Aging, "debunks the traditional assumption [not mine!] that aging and forgetfulness go together." But the "tips" supplied in many recent articles give me a chuckle. They tell you not to worry — all you have to do is "pay attention," "concentrate," "focus on facts." They're absolutely right, but again, none of them tell you *how!* Well, I'm doing that for you.

My white hair was jet black (and all there) when I wrote my first book on memory training. I have to admit that my *natural* memory is not what it used to be. (The old gray mare?) I'll stumble over words here and there, and do the things most people do when they are older. But when I apply my systems, I still can remember anything better, faster, easier, with more retentiveness, than *anyone* — no matter what his or her age. So can you.

And yes, you *can* teach old dogs new tricks — at least, I know I can teach older *people* new tricks. *Even after they've suffered a stroke.* Here's part of a letter I received from Bob Norland of Temecula, California:

> I am a man in my seventies. I had a stroke that paralyzed my right side. What mainly concerned me was that it had affected my mind. We are given the impression that the memory is the first to go, and that it is a function of age. So — while in the hospital, I learned your memory systems.
>
> I'm happy to report that they sure worked. My memory functions now better than it did when I was a young man. I have since given a successful memory demonstration before my local Toastmasters Club. I have no trouble remembering telephone numbers, which is a blessing because I cannot write with my right hand, so when I'm given a number over the phone I have to

remember it because I can't write and hold the phone at the same time.

I was one of those "I can't remember names, but I never forget a face" people. Now I seldom have trouble with names. Thanks to your systems I have now regained confidence in my mind and memory.

All knowledge and all memory is based on associating new information, new ideas, to things and facts you already know. So, you see, the older you get the more you know and the more you've remembered, the more of a *base* there is onto which to connect new things. It's really an automatic process.

If you've worked along with me up to here, you have no choice but to agree that you *can* remember better than ever before — and I don't care *how* old (or young) you are. Do bear in mind that as you grow older your *interest* (not your memory) may start to wane. You don't *listen* as attentively as you used to because you're not as interested. It's important to realize that my systems *force* interest; simply trying to apply them to any kind of material *enlivens your interest* in that material.

On the morning of the day I wrote this, I underwent minor surgery. The anesthesiologist came to talk to me for a moment and introduced himself — Dr. Majithia (an Indian name, pronounced "ma-*gee*-thee-a"). Well, there's no way I'd automatically remember that (because of my age, and because of the circumstances). I'd ordinarily not even hear it. But — I applied my system. I simply pictured myself leaving my mother; I said, *"Ma, gee — see ya!"* That's all. It *forced* me to (a) listen to the name, (b) think about the name, and (c) get its syllables in the correct sequence. *True* memory told me that "see" was pronounced "thee" in this name (I could also have visualized myself lisping; that'd work just fine) and that the accent was on "gee."

I just mentioned "true" memory, as I have a few times previously; I'd better define it. True memory is the associative process with which you're born. As you mature, it's the process that makes you think *white* when you hear "black," think *hot* when you hear "cold" — in/out, up/down, and so forth. It's the process that opens the floodgates of memory. Think of your first boyfriend or your first girlfriend and experiences and other friends from that time flood in. A favorite old song, of course, will do the same. Think of the first time you saw, say, *Gone with the Wind,* and again, that associative process starts — you'll think of who you were with, where you were living, and more. The same is probably true when you think of the moment you first heard that John F. Kennedy had been shot.

So there's true memory and trained memory, and a very thin line separates the two. As you continue to use my trained-memory systems, that line starts to fade; it gets thinner and thinner. Your mind already is an *associating machine.* I'm not giving you anything new, I'm just improving to an incredible degree what you already have!

The way I handled the name Majithia is exactly how I teach mature people to exercise their minds — *every* time they meet someone new. The end result is obvious. I called Dr. Majithia by name in the operating room, and he was shocked (pleasantly) that I remembered it at all, let alone pronounced it correctly. He treated me with a bit more respect and care, I think. But I want you to realize all the other good things you'd be doing in the process of applying my systems that perhaps are *not* so obvious. You would *listen;* most people don't. You would be *thinking,* pinpointing your concentration, registering information in the first place, at that moment (original awareness). You'd be using your *imagination;* and you'd be showing interest — you'd be *impressing* the other person. Most people don't!

The cross I've had to bear (the cross of Lorayne?) for years is that *everybody* knows that physical exercise is good for you. Sure it is; but mental exercise is just as important, if not more so. Using your mind, imagination, concentration — *memory* — can be considered mental sit-ups. And they are easier to do than physical sit-ups. As a matter of fact, many people have told me that they go over, review, some of my ideas (like the Peg Words, or forming a Link of that day's errands) *as* they jog, do sit-ups, and push-ups, ride the stationary bicycle, row merrily along on the rowing machine, or work out in the gym. They tell me that it relieves the *boredom* of the physical exercise. Well, good. But what's more important is that the mind as well as the body is being exercised.

I see commercials talking people into plastic surgery. Face-lifts, body-lifts, buttock tightening, to make one look and, presumably, *feel* younger. A "mind-lift" will definitely do the latter. *Apply* my systems — you'll clear out, refresh those brain cells!

Most mature people want to get ahead, reach higher plateaus, more powerful executive positions. Others may just like what they're doing, but want to become or continue to be the *best in the world* at what they're doing.

George J. Konogeris is Senior Vice President of Kinney Shoe Corporation — way up there on the corporate ladder. He told me:

> Someone with an exceptional memory, young or old, would certainly come to my attention, and he or she would be looked at closely for promotion. A good, strong sales personality usually also has a good memory — they go hand in hand — this holds true for young and old.

Cartier, Inc., has 143 stores around the world and is probably the most famous name in jewelry. Chairman **Ralph Destino** told me:

> The single most successful selling person in our company — I'm putting all our stores together — is one fellow, seventy-six years old; he is by far the best there is. Why? He has a great knowledge of — remembers everything about — gems. So he can speak intelligently about them. That knowledge, however, is almost worthless unless he can sell one of those stones to somebody. *That's* what he does — sells.
>
> He remembers everyone's birthday or anniversary, children's and grandchildren's birthdays. More than that, he'll remember that Mr. X bought his wife a sapphire brooch on their tenth anniversary. Ten years later, he knows it's the twentieth anniversary and he'll call Mr. X to tell him that he has the most wonderful pair of earrings to go with that brooch "you bought for your wife ten years ago"! And, he addresses clients by name, asks about family by name. He has *for sure* made himself indispensable; he is a fantastic salesman (which is just what he wanted, and wants, to be).

That man has made himself indispensable. You can too. Your incredible memory for business details can do it, can give you that much-needed *edge*. Apply these memory systems to become the proud possessor of a most prodigious memory, and for easy, *automatic,* mental exercise.

Other exercises in the areas of creativity, out-of-rut-thinking, problem solving, and decision making can be both fun and valuable. There are some coming up. You can also set up your own exercises, you know. Easily. I've taught you how to think up Substitute Words or phrases for names. I've also taught you how to memorize things in sequence (the Link System). Get a list of the presidents of the United States and memorize them in sequence! The exercise is in the thinking up of the Substitute Words and the forming of the ridiculous pictures. Try to memorize all the states and their capital cities. Or countries of the world and their capitals. You'll learn something — even though you may not be interested in the specific topic — and the *mind exercise* is great.

Before I give you some additional creative-thinking exercises, here are the solutions to Test 7 on page 31. If you haven't tried to solve them yourself, do so now — before you look at the explanations below. Exercise your mind.

a. If you kept those "thinker blinkers" on and thought *only* in terms of Roman numerals, you didn't solve this one. I never said that the answer had to be a Roman numeral. To think creatively is to think *outside* the usual perimeters. The even number involved is six (6 and 8 were the only possibilities). And the solution is to put the symbol "S" in front of the "IX" to get "SIX."

b. You may consider this a "groaner." If you do, I'm sorry. But now you can give your business acquaintances a groan or two. To make the line shorter, draw a *longer* line beneath it. Now the original line is shorter. Isn't it?

c. The problem:

Move only *two* matches to bring the olive *outside* the martini glass. Solution: Slide the horizontal match *halfway* to the left, like this:

Then move the match that's still at the right, near the olive, to the left as indicated by the arrow, to make it the left side off the upside-down glass. You end up with this:

Those mind exercises did make you think, didn't they? Now, can you think of a way to add 2 to 11 and get the legitimate answer of 1? Think about it — think creatively, *outside* the usual perimeters, perhaps along the *peripherique,* as the French would say. Solve it, or give up — then . . .

Try to solve this:

It's an oldie, but if you don't know it, it'll test your creative-thinking ability. The problem? Connect all the dots with only *four* straight lines. (It's easy to do with five lines.) Do it without lifting your pencil from the paper and without touching any dot more than once.

Fill in the letter that's next in this series:

OTTFFSS__

Arrange ten coins (pennies, nickels, or dimes) as shown below.

Consider the arrangement to be an arrowhead pointing up. Move only three coins (which numbers?) to different spots and thus make the arrowhead point *down*.

Where would the next letter go — above or below the line? Why?

<u>A   EF HI KLMN</u>
  BCD   G   J   O

I love the next two riddles:

A man arrives in a small town; he wants a haircut. There are only two old-fashioned barbershops in town. The man looks into one shop and sees that the owner/barber has a terrible haircut, needs a shave, is generally disheveled. The man checks out the second shop; that barber has a great haircut and is clean-shaven. The man goes back to the first (disheveled) barber for his haircut. Why?

A house painter has to paint consecutive numbers, 1 to 100, on one hundred doorways. How many 6's must he paint altogether?

Solutions to these seven mental exercises will be found later on.

Here's another good thinking exercise: Form as many words as you can, within a specific amount of time (two minutes, for example), from the letters of another word. Example: Try to form at least twenty-five two-, three-, and four-letter words from "wearing." Then look at the following possibilities (there are still more!):

wear	an	wean	wen
ring	gear	ran	gnaw
ear	rig	grew	wan

are	age	gain	raw
era	awe	rain	war
we	near	wave	win
in	ire	new	wing

Got the idea? Now try these words (one at a time, of course): practitioner, sympathize, comfortable, cleaning.

A particularly good mental sit-up is to try to join two unassociated items within these specific guidelines: Skip from one word to another by adding a letter, removing a letter, or changing a letter. Also, by using a synonym or antonym, a word that rhymes, or any logical skip from one word to a word that the first one makes you think of. Here's an example: *key* to *book.*

key, keg, wood, paper, page, *book*

or

key, keg, peg, pen, paper, page, *book*

How about *book* to *fish?* Short way — one skip — *book,* hook, *fish.* Longer way: *book,* look, see, sea, *fish.* Try these on your own:

scissors to *pen*

wristwatch to *lamp*

car to *paper*

glass to *hand*

Don't let your mind atrophy — *use* it. The thinking exercises I just described are excellent; applying the systems I'm teaching you is better.

So, learn and apply my systems and stop worrying about growing older. And, remember, when anyone, any group, any corporation, anywhere in the world, wants a memory-training specialist — as a keynote speaker, or as a consultant, or to conduct training seminars — they come to the "old gray mare." *Me!*

In 1983 **Victor Sperandeo,** Managing General Partner of Hugo Securities Company, was the subject of a five-page cover story in *Barron's*. More recently (September 27, 1987), *Barron's* ran a six-page story on Victor headlined "The Ultimate Wall St. Pro." When I interviewed him, Victor said:

The ability to produce wealth comes from knowledge of what is demanded. Your techniques are a method for acquiring knowledge, Harry. Knowledge and memory are the essence of making money.

17

How the Ultimate Wall Street Pro Turned Memory Power into Money-Making Power

Victor Sperandeo started life as a poor kid; he's a self-made man. He was a $65-a-week quote boy at age twenty. Within two years he was trading options for himself. And within four years he was a professional money manager — managing his own money. Victor considers himself a professional speculator. According to a *Barron's* headline, he "goes where the action is; a man for all markets."

"Speculators" speculate with *knowledge*. As you'll learn from this interview, Victor probably speculates with more knowledge than most. Listen as he tells how he got into the trading business in the first place. His attitudes about using memory (for facts, for speeches, for general knowledge) in his business match my own.

VS: I became successful by using my memory. I learned your systems back in 1964/65. I was just out of high school, going to college at night. I wasn't sure what I wanted to do for a living. I read that a biologist, a physicist, and Wall Street trader all made $25,00 a year — the highest-paid positions then. I wasn't good at biology or physics; I was interested in and pretty good with numbers, and I like to gamble; so I chose trading.

In those days there was ticker tape. You had to know what those three-letter symbols that ran across the tape stood for. There were about sixteen hundred issues trading on the New York Stock Exchange.

In January 1968 I was interviewed for a job. I was asked, "What makes you think you can be a trader?" I said, "Well, I've memorized all the symbols on the New York Stock Exchange." I had done it with your systems; I really thought I had to know them to be a trader. The interviewer didn't believe me; he tested me on some little-known symbols. I got every one right. He thought I was a genius and hired me on the spot.

All it really was was that I had an interest and I used your techniques to develop that interest. I saw how impressed people were. It took me about a week to learn the systems and another week to memorize all the symbols. And I was in business! I made about $30,000 my first year (after serving my time as a quote boy); not bad for 1968. Two years later I was making over $50,000 and then I started my own business. I now own three seats on the American Stock Exchange. That's how memory was important to me, in starting a successful career. I don't think remembering symbols is that important now. The concept, the *ability,* is.

I occasionally deliver speeches, and I find I can command respect by hitting my listeners with so many facts that it seems impossible. That's how memory helps me now. They think I'm much brighter than I probably really am. I used to trade everything, so I knew all the symbols and I tried to memorize the prices as the tape moved. You still have to memorize a great deal, although a broker today can look up the symbols.

It's a question of commanding respect. The more you impress, the more business you'll do. From any angle. Impress, command respect, and in this business people are ready to invest money with you, trust you. The ability to rattle off information, memorize whatever you want to, that's how to gain confidence. Had I not memorized all those symbols all those years ago, I probably wouldn't have gotten my first job in the business — a thousand people were interviewed for it. I impressed the guy with only that one thing.

In my experience, Harry, the key to memorization is the ability to understand what you want to learn, of course, and the ability [once you've memorized something] to show it to and impress someone else, especially if it's a large, difficult thing to learn. Your systems make things very clear and easy to memorize. And then there's knowledge. Your memory is your building block to knowledge. If you memorize information, especially if it's a tremendously diversified amount, it's like a computer, you're gathering information you can use in the future. I use your techniques to memorize things I want to retain, things I want to become part of my knowledge.

You're building knowledge and also your intelligence, IQ. You need to keep these things in your memory, even uninteresting information. (That's something you talk about often, Harry.) You have to memorize these things — to get the job, impress people, or just to know it, which was the case for me. I needed to know it; I needed to impress people.

I still know all those symbols after twenty years. I build on that information. Anytime I need to learn something that's diverse, large, new, difficult, I use one of your techniques. It's not only learning for now, it's also learned for the future.

HL: You're agreeing with me that intelligence and IQ are based on prior knowledge, on memory.

VS: Absolutely. Some will disagree, but I believe we're born with a "clean slate." So, as babies we see and learn precepts. You see a tree; you're told it's a tree. Now you have a concept. You now know what a tree is, and that's how the building blocks develop. From that you learn that trees are made of wood and you build tables with them, and that's how you develop your knowledge. Once you learn something, or you ask a question — once something becomes knowledge — you can build on that knowledge.

I've developed a tremendous amount of intellectual ability by using your systems to integrate into my mind things that would otherwise have taken me many years to learn because I don't have a great interest in them, because it doesn't come naturally. I can now learn very quickly. The point is that memory has a great deal to do with IQ and furthering knowledge.

HL: Vic, do you use notes when you deliver a speech?

VS: I want to look at my audience. So I don't use notes, and I refer to many aspects of stock market history, mostly numbers. I can quote the Dow Jones averages through history, without notes, lots of statistical analysis. Most people can't remember numbers, so I impress the heck out of them.

I use analysis and probabilities as do life insurance companies. I know the probabilities in my business. What's the median length of a primary market movement? Go back to 1897 and measure — it's 120 days. That tells you *generally* what to expect. Like an insurance company wants to know if the insured is twenty-two, or seventy-two with a cold. It's changed now to 116 days. So, if the market has been going up for, say, 114 days and you see signs of a cold, you don't want to get 100-percent invested. I have memorized these important numbers, which I use in my speeches.

From December 31, 1986, to May 5, 1987, the market moved from 1896 (Dow Jones — I'm rounding) to 2446 (rounding) and topped on April 6. That's up 550 points. That's about 110 days that the market moved up — about 24 percent. Well, you've got a seventy-two year old man. It *may* go up another 116 days, but prudence dictates — just ask an insurance company what they'd do with a seventy-two-year old man. They don't think he'll live to a hundred; the premium goes up accordingly. That's what I do. In this example, around March 26 to April 6, I got very bearish for just these statistical reasons. The market moved down to 2200; I caught that sell-off, went short, and made a lot of money — using these statistics that I memorized and also use in my speeches.

That's all I'm stressing here. I can't teach people how to trade stocks in this interview, obviously. There's much more you have to know. But having all these statistics at my fingertips makes me look like a guru to most people. I've used your systems for many things; they help me remember everything easily, and with clarity and accuracy.

Let's face it. It seems like I know what I'm talking about when I can go through 130-odd years of history mentioning dates of economic troughs and peaks, et cetera.

You know, I use my own money to trade. Most people in the market make money from commissions. They use other people's money. If the market goes up they make money, if it goes down, too bad, but they still make money. The point is, how do you get that money from other people? You gotta impress somebody. With what? With knowledge! With expertise. Results have to come afterward. I have a stockbroker friend who jokes, ''Give me two million dollars and I'll make you a millionaire!''

Okay. I've used your systems to help me gather the tools I need to be successful in my business. To remember all those numbers — and numbers are difficult to remember, even if you love them!

HL: Is remembering names of people important in your business?

VS: I do meet people in high places, and then I do apply your system to remember them. But I sit in front of computers most of the day. I'm more or less a hermit in business; I don't meet many people.

, You know where I apply your system? I want to know the name of a telephone voice. I have a direct connection to the Chicago Stock Exchange. When I'm called, I want to recognize the voice and call it by name immediately. And the same with many other telephone voices. It saves time. I can lose or gain, say, $600 in thirty seconds. If I have to say, ''Who is this?'' it can cost time and money.

When I'm introduced to someone who I think is important, I certainly use your technique; it works, and the name stays with me. When I meet him again, it's prestigious, it makes me a friend, when I know the name. Wall Street is a small place, and you never know when you'll need friends.

HL: What should I include in my book to help young people, just starting, reach your level of success, Vic?

VS: Once a person has the desire to succeed, he or she has to memorize (learn) everything he can about his business. Then he can expand on that. That's what I did. People must know how to memorize large quantities of information, to program their minds as they program a computer. Get the information in; get it out when you need it. And how to make remembering [learning] fun. . . .

In which area would I like a photographic memory? Numbers, history. I think anyone in the financial area has to give you that answer. When money is entrusted to you, your client wants to know, "How knowledgeable is this person?" On Wall Street it's a referent to history. Because if you know what happened in the past, if you know *how* and *why* it happened — you know more than others. Example: You should know that, historically, whenever a president died in office the market has gone down, especially if it was an assassination, starting with Lincoln. And it has always gone higher within three weeks. So, as soon as news of a president's death is known, the market goes down. Three weeks later, it's higher than before. That's happened each time, without exception. (Sometimes it goes higher in days — but safe side, three weeks.) The point is that if you're handling someone's money, and you have this kind of knowledge, you're more likely to make an intelligent decision based on the past — history, and your knowledge of it.

Victor Sperandeo is a prime example of what can be accomplished when the memory systems are used. He is a prime example of the importance of an exceptional memory in business. For him it was instrumental in getting him "seated" on the American Stock Exchange — three times!

HL: How do actors remember new lines when working in a play?

Charles Nelson Reilly *(Actor, Director):* Because that's what they do. You can tell me to run into the cockpit of a 747 and fly that plane, but I don't know how to do that. Remembering new lines? That's what we do. *It's habit.* When I was doing *Hello, Dolly!* they'd slide new songs under our doors at 11 AM for that day's 2 PM matinee! We did the new songs, memorized them. You know what it is? It's habit!

HL: You know what I think, Charles? I think you have a great memory for lines because you say it's easy, you don't make it a problem.

CNR: Well, that's right. It's what I do — you know what I'm saying? It's still habit! Roberta Peters knows some operatic roles in three languages. In an emergency, she could sing *Fledermaus* in Italian, German, or English. She has sung *La Traviata* in Russian, and can do it in Italian or English. She's been learning opera from the time she was fourteen. It's a habit.

18

Razor-sharpen That Business Edge: Numbers

Prices, Style Numbers, Stock Quotations,
Financial Data, Telephone Numbers,
Intercom Numbers, and More

We are so number-oriented in today's world that I feel we'll all just *be* numbers soon. One problem with that is that in large cities, in busy butcher shops or bakeries, you'd have to *take a name!* (Just a silly joke.) My point is that we are *so* number-oriented that it seems redundant to tell you again how important it is to remember them. We live in a capitalistic society; things are rated by, judged and valued by, the *price* the consumer has to pay for them. When I was in Manila, the Philippines (before Aquino), I found out that the country was under marshal law. I don't know whether one thing has anything to do with the other, but every hotel room — from terrible to great — cost the same number of pesos per night. Not so here in the United States. So prices, telephone numbers, and financial data must be remembered.

I asked **Ralph Destino** of Cartier, Inc., "If I could give you a photographic memory in one area, which would you select?"

> I'd select numbers. Nowadays, in this business, numbers are so important: price of gold — up or down; price of diamonds — up or down; rates of exchange — dollar to franc, pound; interest rates; and so on. I can check these things, but I'd like to have them at my command, and not have to look them up in the *New York Times* or the *Wall Street Journal*.

The late Richard Himber, a well-known orchestra leader (and a personal friend of mine), was the first person I knew of who had a telephone number that matched his name. Some twenty-five years ago, he'd tell people, "Just dial R. HIMBER." There was an RH (RHinelander) exchange, RH 4. His full telephone number was RH 4-6237 (IMBER on the telephone dial is 46237). Richard told me how important this was for him; no one ever forgot his number. Now, especially with the advent of the toll-free 800 exchange, *everyone* wants his number remembered. So, a gourmet strudel baker's number could be 800-STRUDEL. Or, a stop-smoking program's number could be 800-NO SMOKE. A doctor who specializes in hernia operations may advertise and ask you to dial 1-800-RUPTURE! Well, in this chapter, I'll show you how to remember telephone numbers — *any* telephone numbers — plus how to solve many other number problems.

> **J. K. Hartman:** It instills confidence to spout facts and figures seemingly off the top of your head. Even if you're *wrong* (although not in my business; can't be wrong there). That was a John F. Kennedy technique. He'd spout statistics — might have all been baloney, but it sure made you think he knew what he was talking about.
>
> He knew the importance of making it look as if he had a great memory, and thus instilling confidence. He did it during his Nixon debates. He'd rattle off statistics on the number of rockets we had

versus the Russians, and so on. Sounded terrific. Much of it was later proved to be totally incorrect! But it made the necessary points for him. Coming up with statistics — showing off your great memory — is an important part of making an impression in *any* area. Teach us to do it and spout *correct* statistics.

Stephen Rose *(Chairman and CEO, AC and R DHB and Bess, division of Ted Bates Advertising):* Remembering numbers and their relationships, facts, impresses potential clients; it makes credible what you're saying. It's urgent.

Not only does my system for remembering numbers work beautifully, it's also fascinating, imaginative, fun, and *impressive.* You can soar with this technique. (Modesty is a drag!) And you already know it.

You know the Phonetic Number/Alphabet, and that's what's most important. You'll use the Peg Words too, but the sounds are the key. I know that it isn't often necessary to memorize *long* numbers. But students of mine have told me that knowing things like credit card numbers, driver's license number, passport number, and so forth have been life-savers on occasion, and *time*-savers often. Anyway, I want to teach you how to memorize long numbers, because it will be like swinging three bats to make it easier to swing one. Go slow with this chapter. Everything is easy, but it's a new way of thinking for you.

My American Express card (*platinum;* I told you — modesty is a drag) number consists of fifteen digits. Look at this number (it's not my real number; I may be short, but I'm not stupid!): 271384743031050. The principles you've already learned can be applied in order to memorize it. You're going to form a Link of *things,* thoughts or actions, and those things will *tell* you the digits! Because — the words in the Link will contain the consonant sounds that can represent *only* the vital digits according to the Phonetic Number/ Alphabet.

Start your Link with, say, an American flag, to *tell* you that what follows is your American Express number. Then, and this is what first came to *my* mind, Link "flag" to **naked mover crams my tassles.** Now, I can picture that and it will work. It is, however, a "story," which I don't usually use in place of separate associations. But I *saw* it, so I used it. *Separate* pictures, like "flag" to **naked**, naked to **mover**, mover to **creams**, creams to **meats**, meats to *lace* (Peg Word), would probably form a more definite Link in your mind. (A naked person waving a flag, a moving van [mover] is naked, a moving man drinks many creams, creams are poured over meats, a gigantic piece of meat is wearing lace.)

271384743031050

naked mover crams my tassles

naked mover creams ham tussles

nicked my fur grooms ma tousles

nagged move rye crumbs aim toss less

nagged mover crams him teas loss

neck time off rocker miss meat solace

no cat my fur crimes mud slows

Study all of my suggestions above so you can see and learn some of the different ways to go. (You'll need only one way.) Note also that there's no rule as to how many digits should be covered by a word or phrase. Use what comes to mind, cover as many digits at a time as you can. And I usually pluralize to get the **s** for zero into a picture. Think about this. Do you see *why* it works, why it's such a *great* idea?

You can visualize an American flag being carried or waved by a naked mover who crams my tassles, but you can't visualize 271384743031050.

Yes. Numbers have always been difficult to remember because they're intangibles — can't be seen in the mind's eye. But now I've made them tangible for you, and they *can* be seen. Certainly you can see, visualize, or picture *naked*. Well, because of the Phonetic Number/Alphabet that's *got* to represent 271, *nothing* else — no decisions or choices. And so on through the remaining twelve digits of the number.

Diners Club card number 96273212140074. Start your Link with "diners" (people eating). If you want to memorize the number on your own, go ahead. Then, turn the page to check how I did it.

pushing   mountain   dresses   car

9627   3212   1400   74

Everything falls into place. A *four-word* Link *tells* you a fourteen-digit number! There's another standard here: for 27, I try to use the "ing" ending. Add an "er" when you can for a 4. Any of the following would also tell you this number:

pushin' common tinter sis car

bash in come on down there sews core

badge income no tan tires scare

push ink mine down tears screw

I'm giving you multiple examples only to familiarize you with the idea. All you need is one Link. Simple substitution concept. Use the correct *sounds,* to represent the correct digits, and a simple Link will enable you to memorize (forward and *backward,* if you're so inclined) a number consisting of thirty or more digits — in minutes!

A passport number consists of a single letter and seven digits. (Mine does, anyway.) Try F1690143. See *half* (F) of a passport. You touch it up (**touch up**) in a **storm**. That's all! If you don't try it, you'll be *3027191* (**missing the boat!**). Test 8, on page 32, involved a sixteen-digit number. What was scary to you then should be easy, fascinating, and *fun* now. Please don't continue reading until you take that test again. Frankly, I'm applying the "give the dog a bone" principle — the reward principle. The reward makes you continue. Reward yourself; pass the test.

You should have memorized that number in less than two minutes. IQ tests measure as "superior" an adult who can memorize an eight-digit number fairly rapidly; as a "genius," one who can do the same with a twelve-digit number. You've done it with a sixteen-digit number. There's no label good enough for you! Knowledge (in this case, the Link and the Phonetic Number/Alphabet) enables you to create new knowledge (the long number). And there's no need to tell anyone the pictures you see, so you can use whatever you like, so long as it fits the pattern. People are usually interested in the *result,* not the *method!* (That certainly is so with CEOs and managers — show them *results.*) Now, why don't you try to memorize *your* credit card numbers and your driver's license number?

Well, you've swung three bats. Swinging one — prices, telephone numbers, all smaller numbers — is so much easier. Apply exactly the same system. If you want to remember that gold is $460 an ounce, visualize **roaches** all over gold. Always connect the item to the price; make one remind you of the other. That is *it*. Silver is $7.40 — see **cars** all made of silver. (If you don't automatically know where the decimal point goes, you'd never be interested in remembering the prices anyway!) I usually add a word (a Peg Word is fine) to tell me the cents. $762.15 — **cushion towel** does it; so does **catchin' tail**.

> **Edmond E. Chapus:** We have to have facts and numbers at our fingertips. I have to know what went before so I can give a general idea of what a job will cost the client. If we've used similar, say, tubing before, I know how much it cost then; it may be larger tubing we're discussing now, but remembering what came before enables me to come up with a ball-park figure. The people under me, in offices throughout the country — they have to have the prices in the foreground of their minds. They have to be right. They'd better be right!

> **Arlie Lazarus:** There's a saying in our business — *retail is detail.* Part of that detail is prices. I'd like to be able to walk through a competitor's store and do some comparison pricing. If they see you writing, they can ask you to leave. Yes, it's legal; it's been tested in court. I should hire you to do price checks for me!

Arlie won't have to hire me to do those price checks; he'll do them himself after he reads this book. Do you see how you can stroll through a store and do that? You want to remember that a lawn chair is priced at $7.94. Associate chair to **copper**. If it were $7.84 — **gopher**, or **go far**. Make a strong association and keep strolling. A certain flashlight (same product you sell — that's why you're checking) is $3.52. Associate flashlight to **my line**, or **mailin'**, or **melon**. Review lawn

chair/copper, flashlight/melon, and keep going. Associate, review —
you'll *know* them. Prove it to yourself — don't continue until you've
retaken Test 3 on page 27.

Damn! The line is busy. Okay, wait — count to ten; try it again. Oops,
can't. Forgot the number. Have to dial 411 again. Pain in the neck.
(Remember when there were always directories in public phone
booths?) If the operator says, "The number is 390-9521," and if you
think "**maps plant**" as she's saying it, you won't have to call her
again. Yes, being *really* familiar with the sounds is *key*. Why should
that bother you? Being familiar with the keyboard is key to typing;
being familiar with the controls is key to driving; being familiar with
anatomy is key to being a doctor; being familiar with words is key to
speaking; being familiar with the clubs is key to golf — and on and on.
Why should this be different? Well, there *is* a difference — there are
only ten sound/digit combinations, and you already know them. It's
countless times easier to know these sounds than it is to know a
typewriter keyboard.

Calling from a public booth is not the basic telephone-number
problem, of course. You want to know telephone numbers in general.
In Test 11 (page 36), I tried to give you phone numbers for names,
places, or occupations that could be *pictured*. Now, you've learned
how to picture any name. So, if Mr. Jablonski's number is 625-9940,
you might conceivably see a *long ski* (or *jab long ski*) floating down a
channel (or made of **chenille**); the channel is made up of **papers** (or
party **poopers**?). There's no rule that a telephone number has to be
broken into three- and four-digit groups. Use *whatever* comes to mind,
so long as it fits the "pattern." **Chain ill baby, rice** (or **rose**), would
also tell you Mr. Jablonski's number, *if* you associate a Substitute
Word for "Jablonski" to it. Mr. Walker's number is 746-9025;
associate a walker to **crush** (or **crash**, or **carriage**, or **garage**) to
passin' law (or **pose nail**, or **up snail**, or **bison low**).

But wait — that's a 914 area code. Just put **butter** into your
picture. I use *standards* for area codes. "Butter" is my standard for
914. **Patter, batter, pottery, bitter, biter, putter, boater, pouter** —
any one of these would fit.

Dr. Ames number is (715) 410-2009. My standard for Ames is

"aims." I'd see myself *aim*ing a stethoscope (doctor) at **cattle** (my standard for 715, in Wisconsin), cattle to **rats** to **noses up** (all the rats put their noses up), or to **news soap** or **nice sip**.

That's all there is to it. If you use many out-of-state numbers, the area codes will "fall" into standards for you. I always use **Indian** or **antenna** for 212, **pest** for 901, **bottom** for 913, **rotten** for 412, **retire** for 414, **miser** for 304, **mask** for 307, **ash talk** for 617, and so on. Don't try to memorize my standards; make up a word or phrase for an area code as you need it, and that will eventually become *your* standard. *Read no further* until you've taken Tests 11 *and* 12 again (pages 36–37).

Every corporate headquarters I visited had an intercom telephone system. Somewhere near every telephone was a sheet of paper with a two-, three-, or four-digit number (according to the system) next to a name or department. *Every* executive I interviewed said, "Teach me, teach my people, to remember these damn intercom numbers — you'll save so many man-hours (and stiff necks from looking up at that paper) a year!" How simple it is. Associate Substitute Words for names (of person or department) to a word or phrase that *tells* you the number. Mr. Byrnes is 121 — *burns* to **tent**. Ms. Kessler is 101 — *cast law* to **toast**. Sales department is 1403 — *sails* to **dress me** or **tires me**. Shipping department is 712 — lots of **cotton** is being *shipped*. It's all getting to be quite obvious, isn't it? Sure, because it *is,* and it's easy. Try to remember all the extensions in *your* firm.

Being familiar with zip codes saves lots of time, as anyone in the mail-order business, or any business where lots of mailing is done, will tell you. Visualize Manhattan (*man hat*) riddled with **disease**, and you'll know that most Manhattan zip codes start with 100. Mr. Brown lives at 946 West 95th Street, New York City 10025. Your picture for the name and address might be: you *drown* (Brown) on a **porch** (946) wearing a ten-gallon hat (west) as tall as the *Empire State Building* (New York; or the hat is made of *cork*); the building is ringing a gigantic **bell** (95th Street); the bell **tosses** a **nail** (10025). You can *see* it in a split second, certainly in less time than it takes me to write it. You'll prove that to yourself only by trying it. **Pain visor** — 92804;

mason chair — 30264; scare less — 07450; basket low — 90715; rams chef — 43068 . . .

Stock prices are handled like any other prices. The only difference is that there are fractions involved. No problem. The basic fraction is an *eighth*. Let the last digit (sound) of your word or phrase represent eighths. So, "**cart**" would mean 74⅛. If the price is 92¾, work with 926 (¾ is ⁶⁄₈) — **bench**. Yes, bench *could* mean $926. If you don't know which stock is hovering around $92 and which is around $926, get out of the market! Say Exxon is 47⅛ (I'm making up the prices) — associate *eggs on* to **rocket**. Navistar is 19½ — associate *star* (or *navy star*) to **taper** or to **tapir** (½ is ⁴⁄₈).

Is it important for you to remember the basic numbers on your corporation's balance sheet? Make up a "heading" picture to represent the vital categories — like *sets* or *ass* (donkey) *sits* for "assets"; a bill ($1) lying down — *lie a bill* — for "liabilities"; *quit tea* for (stock-holder's) "equity." A simple fictional balance sheet: current assets (rounded off to millions), $891 million; current liabilities, $127 million; equity, $719 million. Just connect the dollar amount to your heading Substitute Word. An *ass sits* because it **fibbed** (assets, 891). A **tank** rolls over a gigantic *bill* that's *lying* on the ground (127, liabilities). You're drinking tea; **get up** and *quit* drinking *tea* (719, equity).

There are, of course, subheadings within the main areas. If you want to memorize securities, time deposits, accounts receivable, accounts payable, taxes, what have you, make up a Substitute word for each item just as you did above and associate the dollar amount to it. Some examples: *see* (or *sea*) *cure* ("securities"), *clock* ("time deposits"), *receiving gifts* and *pay a bull* ("accounts receivable" and "accounts payable"), *taxis* ("taxes").

Schlott Realtors has many offices. Each has a "speed dial" four-digit telephone extension. Richard Schlott told me how helpful it'd be if, say, the main office staff could remember the name of each branch office (city name), four-digit speed-dial extension, manager's name, and secretary's name. Well, a fairly simple association would do it.

The speed-dial number for the Princeton (New Jersey) office is 1065. A *prince* who weighs a *ton* keeps his **dosage low**. Instead of a sequential Link, you can associate each piece of information to *prince* or *prince ton;* that's your heading picture. The manager's name is Peggy Siebens. The prince *sees bins* full of *pegs*. The administrative secretary is Dolores Palmer. Get *dollars* (Dolores) and *palm* tree or Arnold *Palmer* into your association. Try it; review it once or twice. I think you may be surprised at how *smoothly* all the information is simply *there* for you.

It's important in advertising, publishing, and other areas to know which corporations spend lots of dollars on magazine advertising. You could either make a Link of the Substitute Words for the corporations or, if the dollar amount of advertising is important, Link a word or phrase that tells you that to the corporation. In 1985, National Paragon Corporation was the top spender (in millions) — $56,709; then R. J. Reynolds, $35,898; followed by Philip Morris, $20,895. These three examples should suffice. Associate *parrot gone* or *pair of guns* (Paragon) to **leach kiss bee**; *rein holds* or *rain* (on) *Olds* (Reynolds) to **my love puff**; *ma is* or *full lip* (Morris, Philip) to **nose off bell**. Or, use just the corporation names — a pair of guns rains on an Olds; an Olds has a full lip, and so on.

In banking, you may find it time-saving or impressive to know the interest rates for different types of savings accounts.

money market account = 7.27%

6-month CD account = 8.25

1-year CD account = 8.75

2½-year CD account = 9.10

5-year CD account = 9.43

10-year CD account = 10.10

So — see a *market full of money* and a **king** (727) lives there. Do it; you'll see how easy this is. Associate *shoe* (6 months) to **funnel**; *tie* (1 year) to **fickle**; *half a beard* (Noah, half — 2½ years) to **bats**; *law*

(5 year) to **broom**; and *toes* (10 year) to **tastes**. Test yourself on these (after you've made up and visualized your pictures). I want you to see how well this technique works.

The Vice President of Promotion of a large firm wanted to know the basic prices for next-day (air) delivery by different air freight services for three things — a letter, a two-pound package, and a five-pound package. He memorized this chart in minutes using my systems.

	Letter	2 lbs	5 lbs
Express Mail	$10.75	$10.75	$12.85
Purolator	11.75	23.50	33.00
Federal Express	14.00	25.00	34.00
Airborne	14.00	25.00	38.00
Flying Tigers	30.00	30.00	30.00
Emery	14.00	25.00	38.00
UPS	11.50	12.50	15.50

It's so easy when you know how. Make up a *heading* picture to represent each air freight service, and connect the prices to it. *Eggs press* to **dice kill** (10.75) *twice* (10.75 again); the dice look like **tinfoil** (12.85). *Pour later* to **tight call** (or **tote coal**), to **new mules**, to **mummy**. *Fed her all* to **tire, nail, mower**. A **tire** is being *born* (Airborne); the tire has a gigantic **nail** (or hundreds of nails) stuck in it; a gigantic nail is watching a **movie**.

A *tiger flies* to catch and eat *three* gigantic **mice**. An *emery* board is filing a **tire**, tire to **nail** to **movie**. The prices are the same as Airborne. Associating *both* born and tiger to tire/nail/movie would work as well. A gigantic *ewe* eating an enormous *pea* (on an *ess* curve, if you think it necessary; or *ups* — opposite of downs) to **titles** to **toenails** to **toil less**.

As a frequent business traveler, it helped me to know how to transpose "European" temperatures to "American" ones. So, many years ago, I learned to convert centigrade temperatures to Fahrenheit. My method was not precisely accurate, but it served the purpose. The point is that

I've never forgotten it: Subtract 2 from the centigrade temperature then multiply by 2 and add 30. All those years ago I remembered this formula by thinking, ''No, no, mouse!'' (2-2-30). I knew it had to do with temperature because I first saw the mouse shivering with cold, then perspiring because of heat.

Men's U.S. shoe size 8 is size 41 in Italy. Associate shoe/ivy/rat and you'll *know* it. Such conversions, just like temperature conversions, are useful when on a business trip.

The examples are endless, so I'll just have to stop. To go into my examples more deeply would be a waste of time because each one may not hit home for you. My goal is to teach the *concept*. That's easy here. Once you know how to make a number and a name meaningful, and how to make associations, the rest becomes obvious — doesn't it?

HL: From your position as a hirer/firer, are you impressed by a terrific memory? Would such a person come to your attention?

Phyllis Barr *(Administrator, Pavia and Harcourt, law firm):* Absolutely. I'm impressed by anyone who has a terrific memory. Such a person can save the firm money.

Arthur Levitt, Jr. *(Chairman, American Stock Exchange):* Certainly a person with a remarkable memory would catch my attention. That person can be quite valuable to me. I would imagine he or she can be valuable in any business.

19

Meetings of the Mind

*Leave a Meeting with All the Facts
in Your Mind (Remember What You Hear
the First Time You Hear It)*

Many top executives told me that large firms judge new young people by how they do at corporate meetings. Are they too laid-back? Too aggressive? Not aggressive enough? Do they know what's going on? Do they show enough potential for power? Do they show enough interest to remember the important points discussed or made *during* a meeting?

But how you handle yourself at a meeting is important whether you are a new young person or a seasoned senior executive.

HL: You said "memory is power." Would you break that down for me?

Phyllis Barr: A friend of mine is very much into power. Not in terms of money but in terms of controlling people in business. When this person has a business meeting, I'm told, he gets up at 4 or 5 AM to study his notes because he feels it's important to *know* every bit of that information. He memorizes the numbers, all the information, because he can control everyone in that room with memory — knowing all that information and being able to throw it out immediately.

HL: Are you saying that if you know all the facts better than anyone else, that's power? Control?

PB: Absolutely. You can control everyone in the room. Memory is power — absolutely.

I asked most of my interviewees how they felt about taking notes at meetings. Some of the replies:

Alan Greenberg: Well, if everyone had a memory like yours, Harry, I'd rather they looked at me and made eye contact. I'd like people to remember what I said so that they don't have to carry those yellow legal pads around with them wherever they go.

Ellen Hassman: It's vital that I *remember* what's going on at a meeting. I have to be totally aware of my client's problems. I don't take notes; if I do, my concentration is on the writing, not what's being said. I can't write and absorb what's going on at the same time. So I have to listen very intently. Three months later I can discuss the problem without looking at notes. That impresses the heck out of clients, and it also helps me do my job — I'm becoming *imperative* to that client.

Saundra Malvin: Since I want to be sure my staff knows the important points, I like to see them taking notes. And, of course, you're right — if they lost those notes, they'd have to remember those points.

HL: Do you think that the writing of notes enforces memory?

SM: Well, making a mental note of something you've heard — that's once. Writing it is twice. Yes, I believe writing is enforcing memory. By that time I really remember it. I use writing as an aid to, an enforcement of, memory — not as a substitute for it.

Without exception, *every* executive with whom I spoke felt just as Saundra Malvin did about using writing as an *aid* to memory rather than as a substitute for it. **J. K. Hartman** said, "As I write or type, I'm forced to concentrate," while **Ralph Destino** put it this way: "If I relied solely on the paper, I'd be vulnerable. But I find that my direct involvement — writing — completes the memory."

Well, of course! *Just* writing means that the information is going from its source directly to the paper; that information is not registering in your mind at all — it never even *visits*. That's bad. Trying to remember as you write — that's good. But, back to meetings specifically, and other opinions about note-taking.

Arthur Levitt, Jr: I love it when people take notes.

HL: Because you feel that that way they won't forget?

AL, Jr.: That's right.

HL: Again, Arthur, you're placing importance on remembering — remembering what you say during the meeting.

AL, Jr.: That's correct.

William Seco: I'd like my people to remember what I say at meetings so that I don't have to say it more than once.

Joseph V. Casale: I don't want my people to take notes. I'd rather they listen, pay attention, and understand. I don't want to wait while they write.

Gerald S. Deutsch *(Attorney and CPA):* My business activities consist primarily of acting as a tax and financial adviser to my clients. In the course of these activities, I have many meetings with these clients, their representatives, accountants, and attorneys. During these meetings I write as little as possible, because I find that visible note-taking tends to formalize what I prefer to be a relaxed atmosphere with thoughts and expressions freely flowing.

By way of example, during a meeting with a corporate client's insurance broker, his treasurer, and his controller, we reviewed the client's general insurance program. . . .

I'll change names and figures, but the gist of the meeting is intact in the description that follows. I'll explain how my systems can be applied at the same time. The pictures are the ones that come to *my* mind. They will work for you, but your *own* pictures would work much better. The method is basically the same as that for memorizing a speech or sales report, or for remembering facts as you read. The main difference is that the information at a meeting will be more personal, and probably more detailed. In this case, it's a matter of applying the systems to what you *hear,* which, in turn, forces you to *listen* more closely and with more attention and concentration than ever before.

The main points discussed at the meeting were

a. increasing certain insurance coverages;
b. obtaining new, additional, insurance coverages; and
c. determining the company's exposure in certain areas.

See an *ape* stretching, increasing, a cover (see *any* cover — a pot cover, perhaps).

See a *bean* pulling hundreds of shiny new covers close to it, all around it.

Visualize yourself in the *sea, exposed* to the elements.

Inherent to item *a* was increasing the coverage of a certain company building from $3 million to $4 million. To your "ape" picture add the following: the ape is placing your ma ($3 million) over a bottle of rye ($4 million) to *cover* it.

Inherent to item *b* was obtaining leasehold insurance (this covers the loss of good business premises due to a lost lease). The enormous bean has a gigantic *leash* in its hand; it *holds* it tightly. Leash hold — leasehold.

Inherent to item *c* was the client's need for "umbrella" insurance to give him enough liability coverage. You're holding a gigantic *umbrella* over yourself as you float in the *sea*.

After these main points were discussed, assignments were doled out. The *broker* had to

1. obtain a quote from Prime, Inc., a new insurance company;
2. finalize the quote from Gibraltor Company, the client's present insurance company, and see if refunds were due;
3. call in with quotes on leasehold insurance; and
4. increase the coverage of one building from $850,000 to $990,000.

I'd use my Peg Words from 1 to 4 here. See something *broke* or *broken* to remind you that it's the insurance broker's assignment. (You can get that into each picture, if you like.) You're wearing a broken slab of *prime* meat (Prime, Inc.) instead of a *tie* (number 1). You're pulling *oats* or *coats* (quotes) out of the meat.

A large broken *rock* (Gibraltor Company) is on someone's chin instead of a beard (or it has a beard — *Noah,* number 2). You're trying different eyes on the rock, then you attach the *final eyes* (finalize). See the rock giving you a *refund*.

Your broken-in-half *ma* (3) is holding a gigantic leash; the *leash holds oats* — and reminds you of leasehold insurance quotes.

A bottle of *rye* (4) is broken into two pieces. One piece *increases* in size (increase insurance) until it **falls** (from $850,000); the other piece also increases in size — until it **pops** (to $990,000).

The *treasurer* is to review the leases of all the company's stores to determine whether existing insurance coverage is sufficient, considering the changes discussed. He is also supposed to prepare a list of the landlords who must receive certificates of insurance, particularly Maddhat Industries, in Pittsburgh.

Visualize a *treasure* chest. You're looking closely at a lid (reviewing it) to see if it's large enough to cover the chest (sufficient coverage). You're forcing a long line (list) of landlords (people holding buildings in their hands) into the chest. You hand each one a *certificate*. You're *mad* at a giant *hat* that's full of *pits* — as you toss that into the treasure chest.

The *controller* is to go over the company's financial records to check whether *business-interruption* insurance, *fire* insurance, or *loss-of-business* insurance must be increased.

A lion tamer (he *controls* the lions) is running over many (long-playing) *records,* spinning them — they're covered with *dollar bills* (financial records). A gigantic *check interrupts* him, then bursts into *flames*. The lion tamer cries because of the *business* he's *losing*. As he cries, he *increases* in size (to remind you of *increasing* insurance coverage).

As mentioned, the systems are applied as they'd be to a speech, a sales report, or any reading material. Said **Gerald Deutsch:**

> As usual, I sent a detailed memorandum of what went on at the meeting to all participants. The treasurer and controller work with me often, so they expected that memo. The insurance broker had not worked with me before. When he received my memo, he called and, in an awed voice, asked if I'd had a hidden tape recorder working during the meeting!

So you see how very helpful and *impressive* your trained memory can be at business meetings. *Memory makes points!*

Ralph Destino (*Chairman, Cartier, Inc.*)*:* That's Reggie Jackson's bat right there. He's a great friend of mine. Very complex, very complete, very colorful guy. He told me that the secret of his success as a hitter is that he remembers every single pitch thrown by every pitcher in every instance. He says that many players are put down, called "guess" hitters. But he says that in fact, all hitting is guessing, and guessing is really remembering what that pitcher threw to you under similar circumstances in another game. And he stores away all that information.

HL: Just like a pitcher has to remember all the batters' likes and dislikes, has to remember not to throw a particular pitch to a particular batter — because he'll knock it out of the park.

20

Memory
Leads to Creativity —
in Any Business

It takes *imagination,* creativity, to conjure up the crazy pictures needed in order to form strong associations. Imagination and creativity are essential to any career or business. So, I'm really discussing two areas here — the necessity of using imagination and creativity in order to help you form better associations and therefore help you to remember better, *and* the important role that memory plays in helping you to *be* more creative in your own business.

There is a uniqueness here: trained memory is one of the few skills (arts) that automatically *teaches* what is required! It is necessary to use your imagination to form good, strong associations — so you strengthen your imagination because you're *using it more than ever before.* It's automatic. And acquiring an incredible memory will enable you to be more creative where it really counts — in business. What a good, hand-in-hand, Hänsel-and-Gretel tie-in we have here!

Every executive I interviewed for this book strongly asserted that his or her business required creative thinking. And, without exception, each agreed that memory is the key ingredient for stirring up creative thinking. Said **A. S. Clausi,** of General Foods Corporation:

> Of course it's a creative business. My definition of creativity is putting together *previous facts* and/or experiences in new ways to solve new problems or issues. Memory is critical to creativity — that's the data bank that you draw from. To *step out* creatively — keep one foot on the ground. Because if you get both feet off the ground, you'll end up on your ass! That foot on the ground — call it experience, *memory* — that's the data bank. The other foot *uses,* depends on, that foot on the ground.

As I said, every executive I interviewed agreed on the importance of creativity and agreed that memory is necessary for its acquisition. I've never met anyone in a top-level position with any company who *wasn't* creative. Listen again to **Arthur Levitt, Jr.,** Chairman of the American Stock Exchange:

> Creativity is essential. I consider myself to be very creative, and most of my ideas are offshoots and adaptations of other experiences or other ideas that I've used.
> **HL:** You said "experiences." Doesn't that mean remembering all the things you've done or that have happened to you before? Do you agree then, that memory is important for creativity?
> **AL, Jr.:** Oh, absolutely.

I don't believe that anyone is hit with a lightning bolt of creativity in an area in which he or she has no knowledge, no experience. It's only knowledge and experience that can cause that bolt to strike, that thunder to rumble.

Edmond E. Chapus: Creativity is not creating something out of nothing. No, no. It arises because you have a problem to solve, and because you remember similar problems and their solutions. Creativity is based on *memory,* knowledge. When Newton was asked how he came up with the law of gravity, he said, "I was standing on the shoulders of giants!" He, perhaps, saw a bit further than those others *because* he was standing on those shoulders.

I dig the "shoulders-of-giants" concept. Because *I* feel as if I was standing on the shoulders of giants when I started training my memory — to help me get better grades in school, so that my father wouldn't punish me. I had great motivation: *fear.* And I used the ideas and thoughts of men like Aristotle, Plato, Simonides ("the father of trained memory"), Saint Thomas Aquinas, and Shakespeare. Trained memory systems were used by early Greek orators; one such system was the *loci* system of associating thoughts to *places* in one's home. Cicero described how he used memory systems in *De Oratore,* and how lawyers and doctors of his time were aided by, used, memory systems. So in *creating* my memory systems, I really did stand on the shoulders of giants!

Well, you can too. If you've *tried* the techniques I've taught you up to here (some are streamlined versions of techniques used by those "giants"), you're already thinking differently, thinking creatively. You're exercising your imagination by forming associations. And, you can use your newly acquired memorizing ability to become more familiar with "giants" in your own career, your own business. The more familiar you are with those giants, the more you remember of their accomplishments, the easier it will be for you to stand on *their* shoulders and launch your own creativity.

Victor Sperandeo: In order to create, you've had to learn, *know,* something first. Then you expand upon that. My ideas were stimulated by Charles Dow. I memorized all his ideas and created new ideas from and around them. I built on, created with, his ideas. If I didn't know/remember all his ideas, I couldn't have done that. Once I memorized them, they became knowledge. I can build on that.

Creativity is the outcome of memory. Memory is stored

knowledge. I couldn't possibly get a million-dollar idea on how to build a better TV set, because I don't know the first thing about TV sets. But I can possibly get a creative idea on how to make a killing in the market — because I *know* the market.

It's all part of learning, you see. Learning is the gathering of information, data — and there is no learning without memory. There simply isn't. Because "gathering information" *means* remembering that information. How could a medical student become a doctor if he or she didn't remember pertinent medical information? He or she couldn't. Ask any doctor and you'll find out that when you take the exam that can give you the "shingle" — give you the title "doctor" — it's your *memory* that's being tested. And your memory continues to be crucial into "doctorhood."

Dr. Sheldon Lippman *(Pediatrician, affiliated with Maimonides Hospital, Bronx, New York):* To achieve significance in his specialty, a doctor has to be dedicated, of course, but most of all it takes memory. With a great memory one can really make advances in academics, in research. You have to remember the knowledge you've gained empirically, through testing and experimenting. Memory is crucial. I have to remember everything in my field if I want to be creative in my field.

Memory is also imperative for the bar exam that aspiring attorneys must take, and, again, it is needed for creativity in the profession.

Peter Kougasian: All creative thinking is analogy. When you say, "Wait a minute — this is like so-and-so!" it's that jump, that analogy, that brings about creative thinking. But you have to *remember* the so-and-sos. The broader your range of knowledge, the more creative you can be within your profession. Using your systems, Harry, has made me think more creatively!

I can't think of a business where creativity is unimportant, where it doesn't *make money* for that business or company, though it may not be as obvious for some as it is for, say, the advertising business. **Ellen**

Hassman told me that "memory and creativity *must* go hand in hand. The more I remember about a client and his problems, his audience, his markets — and my own business — the more likely it is that creative flash will hit me. And the more likely my company will keep that client, and the more likely I will make more money. Definitely." And **Stephen Rose** said that he finds "memory to be an urgency — it helps to elevate the creativity I have. In order to be creative, you must remember everything that came before."

Memory and creativity go hand in hand in every business. Note the following words, thoughts, of the chairmen of two diversified businesses.

> **Cy Leslie:** Creativity is the construction of something that has not existed, or the improvement of something that has. The *change* of an existing something. In our business, in order to be creative, it is essential to remember what came before. Einstein had to remember the composition of mass, the composition of energy, the mathematical formulas and processes of so many different things in order to come up with relativity. You can't create in a vacuum — there has to be knowledge, and knowledge is memory.

> **Ralph Destino:** Your definition of creativity — the brilliant application or use of accumulated facts — is right on. It's the bringing to bear of a fresh point of view. It would seem to me that a person's creativity is directly related to how well he or she knows what's gone before — and therein lies memory: *accumulated* facts and information. Knowledge — *memory* — is essential for creativity.

Obviously, it pays to be creative, to exercise your imagination. "Imagination," said Henry J. Taylor, "lit every lamp in this country, produced every article we use, built every church, made every discovery, performed every act of kindness and progress, created more and better things for more people. It is the priceless ingredient for a better day."

To repeat then, just forming crazy associations, as you've been doing, is an excellent imagination exercise, besides enabling you to remember as you never could before. *Exaggeration* helps you to create better, crazier, or more impossible and thus more *memorable* pictures for your associations. That same kind of exaggeration can help you come up with crazy, impossible answers or solutions to business-related problems. It's part of *brainstorming*.

If you laugh at some of the resulting answer-solutions or ideas, or if you think, ''Hey, I'll go to jail if I do *that*,'' that's good. *Fantasize*. Albert Einstein said, ''The gift of fantasy has meant more to me than my talent for absorbing positive knowledge.'' You'll come up with more and more answers, ideas. They may not be workable — but then again they may. When you work up lots of crazy ideas, quite often you'll find a gem among them.

If you tried to solve the ''creative-thinking'' riddles in Test 7 and those in chapter 16 (the answers to which follow), again, you've exercised your imagination, your creativity.

If you didn't lock yourself into a thinking rut, you may have solved a few of the mind exercises in the '' 'Staying/Graying' Power'' chapter. For the ''dot'' problem: Who said you had to stay *within* the square formed by the nine dots? *I* didn't. If you locked yourself into that rut, *assumed* you had to stay within the square, you *couldn't* solve the problem. If you brainstormed it, one of your ''crazy'' ideas may have been ''Can I draw some lines *out* of the square?'' Why not? *That's* the solution:

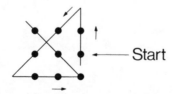

Add 2 to 11 to get 1. Perhaps you thought *only* of numerals, Arabic and Roman. You *assumed* that therein would lie the solution. No way. Had you thought of *time,* you might have realized that adding 2 *hours* to 11 o'clock brings you to 1 o'clock!

''O T T F F S S'' stands for One, Two, Three, Four, Five, Six, Seven! The next letter in the series, obviously (now), is E for *Eight*.

Look back at the ten-coin "arrowhead" problem. Slide coins 7 and 10 up to the left and right of 2 and 3. Move coin 1 down below ("south of" and centered between) 8 and 9. The arrowhead is now pointing *down*.

All the letters above the line (AEFHIKLMN) are formed with straight lines only; the letters below the line (BCDGJO) are not; they also, or only, have curved lines. The next letter in the alphabetical sequence is P. It has a curve; it goes below the line.

For his *own* haircut and shave, each barber would go to the only other barber in town. The disheveled barber obviously gives the better haircut.

The house painter will have to paint *twenty* 6's. You'll rarely get the right answer to this. The usual answer is *eleven*. There's a built-in red herring. Most people will go through the numbers 1 to 100, thinking, "6, 16, 26, 36, 46, 56 . . . aha! here's the catch — *66*. Two 6's here. He won't trick me with *that*." They'll arrive at eleven 6's. The "66" red herring causes them to overlook the 6's in 60, 61, 62, 63, 64, 65, 67, 68, and 69! Try it on a business acquaintance; he or she may have to pick up the check for lunch.

Steven A. Conner *(Owner, Asset Management Planning)*: If I forgot appointments, there's no way I could stay in business. I don't forget them, and I do quite well, thank you. I haven't used an appointment book in four years. I average thirty to forty interviews a week. In those four years, I have *never* forgotten an appointment. I *use* your systems. Each morning, I know exactly where I have to be. It's very much like being a computer — after my appointments that week, I can erase and start all over again.

George J. Konogeris *(Senior Vice President, Kinney Shoe Corporation)*: I sure would like to look at my calendar and definitely remember my week's appointments. Missing just one can create problems.

21

Specific "Day/Hour" Appointments

The Weekly Appointment Calendar in Your Mind!

There's remembering names and faces, there's remembering numbers of all kinds, there's remembering general *business data* — and there's remembering business appointments. All these really do blend together, but the point at this moment is: How could you run a business if you didn't keep appointments?

A. S. Clausi: To me, an appointment is a sacred commitment. And being there on time is part of the measure of you as an individual, and of how well you do things. It becomes a driving, permeating force. I missed a 10:30 appointment today. That bothers me. This day is less perfect for me because I missed it.

Cy Leslie: I think keeping appointments and keeping them on time is very important. Oh, absolutely, absolutely. Some people are traditionally late for appointments; that's distasteful to me. It also upsets other people. I am almost always on time. There are executives who think you ought not to be on time — it looks as if you're not busy. I think that's wrong.

As I said in chapter 7, forming a Link of the things they want to do each day is sufficient for many business people. You *could,* if you wanted to remember a time for an item in your Link, include a word to (phonetically) tell you the hour. You could even include a Substitute Word for a day. But for that kind of appointment — on a specific day and at a specific hour — there's a better way. Because day of week and hour of day are ephemeral, rather than concrete, pieces of information, they're difficult to visualize and therefore difficult to remember. It's the usual problem: How can you make that kind of intangible information tangible? What you need are *specific* compartments, pigeonholes, in which you can store your appointment information. The compartment itself must tell you, must visually *represent,* a day and hour.

Well, you can create those compartments. As a matter of fact, you already have them; you simply have to *label* them — make them tell you the information you need. I'm talking about the Peg Words. For every day of the week and for every hour from 1 to 10 o'clock, your Peg Words will be your appointment compartments. (We'll handle 11 and 12 o'clock later.)

The first thing you have to decide is whether you will consider Sunday or Monday the first day of the week. Calendar-wise it's Sunday, but every executive I interviewed considered Monday the first day of the week because it's the first business day. So I'll teach it that way — Monday, the first day; Sunday, the seventh. When you understand the method, you can change it any way you like.

Assume you want to remember an appointment for Tuesday at 5 PM. One Peg Word can represent that. Tuesday is the *2nd* day and the hour is 5. A two-digit number — *25* — tells you that: 2nd day, 5th hour. Ordinarily, of course, it would have been just as difficult for you to remember 25 as it would be to remember Tuesday at 5. But now it isn't, because you know how to visualize 25; you have a Peg Word that *means* 25: *nail*. What a simple, fascinating, and *workable* idea! *Nail,* within the appointment context, can represent nothing else but the 2nd day (Tuesday) at the 5th hour. Nail is your compartment for Tuesday at 5.

Remember the entity-of-two idea I've talked about. Visualizing Tuesday at 5 (by picturing a nail) is fine, but it isn't too practical until you make nail tell you what the appointment on Tuesday at 5 *is*. How? Well, you know that, too. Associate one to the other, make one remind you of the other. If your Tuesday at 5 appointment is with Harry Printz at Empire Manufacturing Company, you might visualize a *prince* being an *umpire* at a game where *nails* are the players. Oh, yes, it's silly — and oh, yes, it works.

You can insert anything you like into the association. If you want to remember the first name, make the prince *hairy*. The address is 712 Chambers Street. You can see all that hair on the prince being **cotton** (712), or the nails are **cuttin'**. The game is being played in a judge's *chambers,* or get chamber pot or *shame bear* into your picture!

You have to meet Mr. Rybakov for lunch on Friday at 2 PM. You know the appointment is for PM not AM. You can put a word into your picture to represent either — **poem** or **aim**, for instance — but I don't find that necessary. All right; Friday is the 5th day, and it's 2 PM you're interested in; 52 — **lion**. It could be nothing else. If you see a lion eating a *rib* for *lunch* and it makes him *cough* (rib cough — Rybakov), I'll guarantee you won't forget that luncheon appointment.

I'll guarantee it if you will go over the compartments, the Peg Words, for each day every day, or every preceding evening. On Thursday night, you simply think "lot, lion, loom, lure, lily, leech, log, lava, lip, lace" — and when you come to *lion* you'll immediately be reminded of tomorrow's lunch date (at 2 PM) with Mr. Rybakov. Note that I included the Peg Word *lace* (50). That's the compartment for Friday at *10*. Since there is no 0 o'clock, we might as well put that zero to work and make it represent 10 o'clock. So *toes* is Monday at 10; *nose* is Tuesday at 10; *mouse,* Wednesday at 10, and so on — to *case,* Sunday at 10.

Richard Schlott: When I was a salesman I'd write my appointments on a piece of paper. If I forgot an appointment, I'd lose a sale, or annoy somebody. Ah, if only I could have remembered them, with *confidence,* and not have had to worry about losing a damn piece of paper. That would have been great! And it'd be great for all my salesmen *now.*

Now then, 11 and 12 o'clock. There are several ways to go, but I'll teach you what I use because I've found it to be the most sensible. Handle 11 and 12 as you would 1 and 2 but use a word *other than your Peg Word.* That's all. Thursday at 1 o'clock is *rod* (41 — 4th day, first hour). For Thursday at 11 o'clock you can use any word that fits phonetically but is not your basic Peg Word — like *rat, root, rut, rid,* and so on. You'll know that it represents Thursday at 11 o'clock because only *rod* can represent that day at 1 o'clock.

Monday at 2 o'clock is *tin.* For Monday at 12 use *ton, tone, dine, din, tan, tuna* — anything that fits phonetically, except your basic Peg Word, *tin.* That's the system. And you see that knowing your Peg Words (at least into the 70's) is essential.

As appointments for next week come up, form your associations. Then, starting on Sunday night, go over the next day's Peg Words. For Monday — *tot, tin, tomb, tire, towel, dish, dog, dove, tub, nose, toad, ton.* If you've used any of the words in an association, and if you made that association ridiculous, clear, and strong enough, there is no way you can forget an appointment. When you think the compartment word, you'll stop — realize you have an appointment for that time — and you'll also know *what* the appointment is! This has to work, incidentally; all you need do is try it.

I didn't test you on appointments in chapter 4 — my reason being that you knew how bad you were at remembering appointments! But you can test yourself now. Look at these appointments. I've listed them haphazardly, because that's the way they come up in real life. Just figure out which Peg Word represents day/time, then associate that to the appointment. Do this — I want you to gloat over your great memory for appointments.

Wednesday at 1: meet with Mr. Kwitekowski
Friday at 10: dental appointment
Monday at 2: meeting at bank with Mr. Pierce

Wednesday at 5: check hotel room for conference
Tuesday at 9: call Ms. Hopkins
Thursday at 4: flight to New Orleans
Tuesday at 12: meeting with Mr. Ponchatrain
Saturday at 3: golf with the Smiths
Friday at 2: lunch with Bill Talbott — at Guide, Inc.
Monday at 8: sales meeting at home office

If you've made good, strong associations, go over your Monday compartments (the Peg Words and the 11 and 12 o'clock words). Your memory will *stop* at two appointments and you'll know what they are. Then go over Tuesday words — again, your newfound great memory will stop you at two appointments. Do Wednesday and remember two appointments. Thursday, one appointment; Friday, two; and Saturday, one. And you can use the idea every week. It's like a magic slate; use it and it automatically clears the preceding week.

I rarely bother with *minutes* when recalling scheduled appointments. If they're important to you, put a word into your association to remind you of them. If anything, I'll use only 15, 30, and 45 minutes after an hour. The pictures I made up almost half a century ago are the ones I'd use now, because they work perfectly. I get a quarter (25-cent coin) into my association to remind me of a quarter past, a half grapefruit for half past, and a pie with one slice missing (three-quarters of a pie) for 45 minutes past (or a quarter to the next hour).

If you need to remember specific minutes, use a basic Peg Word to represent day and time and a word that fits phonetically but is *not* a basic Peg Word to represent the minutes. This avoids confusion. Example of the *wrong* way to go about this: A picture of a *knob* and *roof* could mean Tuesday at 9:48 *or* Thursday at 8:29. It's the *or* that's the problem. There must be no confusion when applying my systems. *Knob rave* solves the problem. You'd know that the basic Peg Word is the day/hour; the *non*basic word represents the minutes.

"I have to keep calling radio stations to get them to air new releases," **Harvey Leeds** told me. "One of the things in this business is that the program or music directors will take calls only during certain hours of certain days. And each station slots the call times differently. There's a memory problem for you.''

To solve Harvey's problem — remembering the day and time when the music director of a particular radio station will accept calls — you can use a word to remind you of a day of the week and insert a word that tells you the time spread. The words are easy: picture the *moon* for Monday, *dues* for Tuesday, someone being *wed* for Wednesday, *thirsty* for Thursday, *fry* for Friday, *sat* (or *sit*) for Saturday, and *sun* (or *son*) for Sunday. Then, for the hours, don't use your basic Peg Words; use any other word that tells you the time spread, phonetically.

An example: WDIZ in Orlando, Florida, will accept calls only on Thursdays between 3 PM and 5 PM. The association might be: An *oar lands* (Orlando) and gets **dizzy** (DIZ) and *thirsty* (Thursday). It drinks all the **mail** (3 to 5; **mill, male, mull** would also do). You could, if you'd rather, use the letter words for the station — **dean eye zebra.** For any memory problem, use what comes to mind first; that's usually (though not always) best. You can also include a Substitute Word for the music director's name, if you like.

KSPN in Aspen, Colorado, will accept calls only between 8 AM and 10 AM on Fridays. (I'm making up the days and times.) An *asp* (Aspen) is in a gigantic **spoon** (SPN). You hold it over fire to *fry* it (Friday) — and this turns it into a **fetus** or a **fat ass** (8–10).

HL: Evan, what would you like your people to remember?
Evan R. Bell: Among other things, there are the "recurrings." That means that on a certain day of the week, every week, allowance checks are mailed to certain clients. If the account executives could remember which, say, six clients' checks are mailed on Wednesdays, and which on every other day, that'd save oodles of time. It would also help in catching and avoiding computer errors, which do happen. Can you teach my account executives to connect, say, seven names to Monday, six to Tuesday, et cetera?

This should no longer be a problem. One example suffices. Assume that the account executive needs to know that on Wednesdays checks must be mailed to the following clients: Russell, Petrofskya, Lorayne, Mitchell, MacKenzie, Alpert. The heading picture is a *wed*ding — for Wednesday. To that, Link *wrestle* (Russell — a bride and groom wrestle) to *pet rough sky, ah* (people are wrestling on a rough sky, they pet the rough sky, and say "ah") to *law rain* (gavels — law rain from the rough sky) to *mitt shell* (baseball mitts and shells rain down along with the gavels) to *Mack* (truck) *can see* (a Mack truck looks through a mitt and shell [instead of binoculars] and can see) to *all put* (Alpert — all you can find is put into a Mack truck).

The last two problems aren't standard ones. I wanted to show you that, with your new knowledge, it no longer matters what the memory problem is — you can handle it. Most important here is the compartment idea for remembering appointments by day and hour. And now you have those compartments — *forever*.

Richard Schlott *(President, Schlott Realtors — 150 offices, 6,000 employees):* Good sales people *do not forget.* Great sales people obviously do not forget — they never forget *anything.* I mean they don't forget names of potential buyers or specifications of homes or appointments to see or show a property. And they make sales, which they wouldn't do if they didn't have good memories.

William Seco *(Vice President of Sales and Engineering, EDP World, Inc.):* Can't afford to forget; forgetting just doesn't exist in this business — you wouldn't make any money. If an employee forgets to, say, make an important phone call, that's it — he's lost that transaction. You get only one strike in this business. Forgetting costs money.

22

Place That Face!

In Business, You Must Force Each Face
to Tell You Its Name

"Hi, Dr. Smith."

"Oh, hello — uh, er. How are you?"

"That tooth you worked on the last time I was in your office is giving me trouble. I think a piece of crown broke off. Hate to ask you to look at it here on the street, but no one's around right now."

"Oh, sure, Miss — uh, er. Let's see."

"It's this one."

"Ah, Miss *Mitchell*, yes. No problem . . ."

No problem with the tooth, but that dentist sure has a tough time remembering names and faces. He's not alone. We all can remember what we're interested in.

Dr. Smith is interested in *teeth*, in his own work; when he sees *that* he knows the person's name. Out of the office, show a doctor the scar that resulted from the operation he performed and he'll call you (it) by name!

Now, if only they could be as interested in *faces* — if the art connoisseur could be as interested in faces as he is in brushstrokes, if the baseball player could be as interested in faces as he is in pitches, if the collector could be as interested in faces as he is in antiques. If we could all be interested in faces, we'd remember them.

Arthur Levitt, Jr.: This is a people business. I still deal with people, and I'd put remembering names and faces above and beyond anything else. In our society people are too used to being gray intangibles rather than being Harry Lorayne, the great memory expert.

Richard Roth, Jr.: There are so many things to remember in architecture — but if I had to select one for importance, it'd be names and faces. I'm in a selling business. If I'm doing a building where billions of dollars are involved, it's crucial that I don't forget the name of the person controlling those dollars.

Everybody says, "Oh, I recognize faces, it's the names I can't remember." (Did you ever hear it the other way around?) Everybody says it; it's true — and it's meaningless! If you don't know the name, saying "I recognize your face" to the president of your company doesn't move you up a step, does it?

I've repeatedly told you that you have to *force* your mind to attention and pinpoint your concentration. That automatically forces interest. How can I force you to *listen to a name* and *look at a face?* More to the point, how can you force *yourself* to do those two things? That's *all* it takes to remember names and faces.

There are three steps involved. The first is to make up a Substitute Word for the name when you're introduced to a new person. That forces you to *listen* to the name. Think about it. You're introduced to a Mr. Kovechev. If you've made up your mind to apply my system, *talk to yourself:* "I'll have to introduce this person to someone else later, I'd better pay attention." You cannot allow the introducer to get away with a *mumble,* nor can you allow the person to mumble his or her own name. How can you possibly come up with a Substitute Word (*cover chef,* perhaps) if you don't *hear the name?* You can't. That's why even if my systems don't work, *they must work.* You are forced to say, "Sorry, I didn't get the name." You are forcing yourself to do the one most important thing when it comes to remembering names and faces: *hear the name.*

Not only do you force yourself to hear it, but the act of thinking up the Substitute Word forces you to *concentrate* on it for that *fraction of a second* as you never concentrated on a name before. It's painless, and you have *no choice.* Assume then, that you've heard the name, Kovechev, and you've thought of *cover chef.* Great; that's step 1.

Step 2: Select an *outstanding feature* on Mr. Kovechev's face. It can be *anything* — high or narrow forehead; lines on forehead or face; large or small eyes or ears; thin, straight or thick lips; full or sunken cheeks; large, small, or pug nose; wide or narrow nostrils; thick, thin, curved, or straight eyebrows; receding or jutting chin; clefts or marks of any kind. Whatever impresses you on first look. And there's the key word — *look.* In order to select an outstanding feature, you are *forcing* yourself to do the next essential thing: *look at the face.* Looking for that feature *forces* you to get an *overall* look at that face. Again, you're concentrating, without realizing it, as you never have before.

Steps 1 and 2 *must* elevate your memory for names and faces to a new, higher plateau. But you can move it to the highest plateau with step 3. And that is doing what you've already practiced, already learned to do: *form a silly association* between the two vital items! The two items are your "picture" (Substitute Word) for the name, and the outstanding facial feature.

If the feature isn't really *the* outstanding one, it doesn't matter. Use it. *You looked* at the face with concentration — *that's* what matters. Let's really meet Mr. Kovechev at a business cocktail party.

You've already listened to the name; you're thinking *cover chef.* Now look at the face (see page 193, top). Would you select the thick lips or the very bushy eyebrows? There are many choices; assume you chose the eyebrows. Make them *tell* you the name! As you shake hands, form an association. Perhaps you're *cover*ing each eyebrow

with a *chef* (someone wearing a chef's hat). I get violent. I'd see chefs flying out of those eyebrows, tearing them asunder; I'm covering each. *Really see* your picture. Neither the feature you select nor the picture you see is as important as the fact that you're *doing* it at all and that you see the picture *clearly*.

All right; you've met Mr. Kovechev, chatted a while *using* his name. Now you wander off and greet two more new people. Say hello to Dr. Newcombe and Miss Van Nuys.

The obviously outstanding feature on Dr. Newcombe's face is that strong, jutting chin. He also has large earlobes, a high forehead, et cetera. I'd go with the chin. See a gigantic *new* (shiny) *comb* raking that chin, or see that new comb on his face *instead of* the chin! There are stethoscopes (doctor) falling out of the chin — or you're combing with a stethoscope. *See* whatever picture you decide on. Bring your attention to Miss Van Nuys. You've already thought *van noise,* because you *listened.* Now *look.* Well, she has a pug nose. Can you visualize a moving *van* on (or instead of) that nose? And it's making a terribly loud *noise* that you can almost hear? *See* that picture. Chat for a moment.

Now it's time to leave Dr. Newcombe and Miss Van Nuys. You might catch a glimpse of Mr. Kovechev, and his name will come to mind — that's a *review* for you. Think of the name whenever you see the face of any of the people you're meeting. As you turn you bump into the host, who introduces you to (a) Mr. Fleming, (b) Ms. Isaacson, and (c) Mr. Nichols.

a

b

c

Tell your host to *slow down,* if necessary; you want to be sure to hear those names. One way to work it is to say, "You're busy; go on, do your thing — I'll introduce myself." *Don't* let the host or hostess rush you. Okay. Look at Mr. Fleming. You've already *listened* and *concentrated,* and thought of *flaming.* You can use the mustache, the hairline, whatever you like. I'd use the mustache. See it — *really* see it — burning, *flaming.*

Now — Isaacson. *Ice* (or *eye*) in a *sack* will do it. If you like, include *son* or *sun.* You'll find, as you work with this idea, that you don't have to cover the *entire* sound of a name. Remember, all you want is a *reminder.* "Ice sack" *will* suffice.

Look at that high forehead, square jaw, very large eyes. See sacks of ice (*ice sacks*) flying out of those eyes. (Smaller replicas of the sacks would remind you of *son.*) *Ice sacks* (*son*). Force the eyes (or whatever feature you're using) to *remind* you of Isaacson. Be sure to see that picture.

Turn to Mr. Nichols. No problem — *nickels;* coins. No problem with *any* name: Jubaneuski — *you ban new ski;* Lancaster — *land caster;* DeLeon — *the lion* or *deli on;* Simionides — *sigh me on nighties;* Cunningham — *cunning ham;* Kantrowitz — *can't throw wits* (brains); Menninger — *men injure;* Betancourt — *bettin' court* or *bed in court;* O'Neal — the letter *O kneel*ing; Pumphrey — *pump free* or *pomme frites;* Cercelli — *sir sell E;* Babbiarz — *baby R's.*

See Mr. Nichols's straight-across eyebrows, broad nose, large mouth. You might see millions of nickels pouring out of that mouth. That's all that's necessary — but really see it.

Have you made these six associations? I mean, *really?* You've actually visualized the pictures I've suggested, or those you thought of yourself? If you have, you *know* the six people you've just met. Go back; look only at the faces, the names will spring to mind.

Did you know them all? If you had trouble with one or two, *strengthen* your association; that is, be sure to see the silly picture *clearly.* Then — on page 196 they are in different order. Fill in the right names.

When I asked **Cy Leslie** if remembering names and faces is important to him, he answered, ''Remembering names and faces has a long-term *cumulative* effect in business relationships.'' And **Scott Marcus** said that ''remembering the face and name of a client puts you way ahead of the competition. The ability to do that is very important in the marketing end of our business.''

Say you enter a meeting room; there are six new people there. Let me introduce you. Do the rest on your own. And yes, you can use a beard or a hairdo. For Ribykov — *rib (a) cough;* Callahan — *call a hand;* Kendall — *candle;* Mouzalas — *moos* (or *moose) alas;* Bierborn — *beer born;* Prescott — *press cot,* of course. Here they are:

MR. RIBYKOV

MS. CALLAHAN

MR. KENDALL

MR. MOUZALAS

MR. BIERBORN   MISS PRESCOTT

Pretend each one is a real person. Meet them one at a time: (1) think of the Substitute Word; (2) select, look for, an outstanding feature; and (3) *connect* the two. *Really* try it. If you don't, you're not doing *either of us* any good! Once you've made the six associations, you will know the six names and faces — even if you see the people in a different order, like this (put the correct name in each blank):

Did you know them? Of course you did. You've met *twelve* new people. Go back and see if you know all twelve. The worse that can happen is that you'll forget one or two. That's probably better than you've ever done before! *Try it*.

Now, really impress yourself — turn back to chapter 4 and take Test 9 again. *Do not continue* until you've done that.

You now know twenty-four new people. And it's even easier in real life. Try it the next time you meet some people. You'll impress yourself and, more important, you'll impress and flatter the people you meet. And don't let long or foreign-sounding names throw you. All names become easy to handle when you apply the Substitute Word idea.

Phyllis Barr: Remembering names and faces is not only good management — it's essential. It makes the people under you feel important; it motivates people to work harder for you.

Alan Greenberg: Most important area of memory? Faces — names.

HL: If I asked that same question of people under you, people who are interested in climbing that ladder of success — trying to reach *your* level — would they give me the same answer?

AG: If they had any sense they would!

One final example, just to lock it in for you. At a recent speaking engagement I met (among three hundred other people) an Indian gentleman, Mr. Srinivassan. I thought of *serene E fasten,* and suddenly the name was no more difficult than Flanagan (*fan again*)! Try it — meet Mr. Srinivassan:

Look for and decide on one feature. Perhaps the cleft in his chin, or the curly hair. You might see a gigantic *serene E* falling out of that cleft — but you *fasten* it in place.

In business, you may want to review mentally the people you've met during the day. Just think of the face and the name will come to mind, and vice versa, *if* you've applied my system. That's your review. Let some time go by — then see if you still remember the thirteen people you met in this chapter and the twelve you met in Test 9. Won't you be pleasantly surprised when you remember all twenty-five?

Ralph Destino *(Chairman, Cartier, Inc.):* We have a training program, and there are three important things that are covered: (1) product knowledge — how to know your products; (2) nuts and bolts — how to write a sales slip, how to charge, how to handle a credit card; and (3) — more important than 1 and 2 — manner, style. Number 3 is the really *important* thing. Our clients are the tip-top of the economic iceberg of taste, breeding, heritage, et cetera. Those clients expect first-class products — that's where product knowledge comes in. They expect efficient service, that's number 2. And much more than 1 and 2, they expect to be treated accordingly. And that means memorizing their names, knowing who they are. Our clients want to be *known*. People respond to being remembered, recognized.

23

Voices Are People Too

*Recognize and Remember Telephone Voices;
Plus, More "People" Information*

During my interviews with them, both Dr. Sheldon Lippman and Dr. Jesse Manlapaz told me — as have many other doctors through the years — that they'd love to be able to connect a name (and medical problem) to a telephone *voice*. Why? Because they're often called at home by their patients. They'd like to leave the impression that each patient is important.

Not all people are polite enough or thoughtful enough to identify themselves immediately when they run into you unexpectedly or call on the telephone. No, some people thoughtlessly say only hello and let you stew, forcing you to say, on the telephone, "Who's this?" Most executives would simply rather not have to do that; it is an admission of forgetting.

J. K. Hartman: We do *much* business over the phone. It'd be just terrific to be able to say a caller's name before he or she says it. That's as important as connecting a name to a face. It's part of effective communications and relationships.

Alan Greenberg: As you can see, Harry, there are hundreds of people sitting in this room, and most of them are on the telephone. It goes without saying that it's important for them to recognize, remember, voices. It's impressive, it's good business to be able to say, "Hi, Mr. So-and-so," before he *tells* you that he's Mr. So-and-so.

I've taught blind people how to remember voices; that is, how to tie a name to a voice. This ability is important because quite a few blind people do telephone work. It is, obviously, also important in business generally. And because, like faces and fingerprints, all voices are different, it isn't a difficult thing to do.

The principle is the same as the one that works when you associate a name to a face. You need a *hook,* something onto which to hang that name. And just as searching for an outstanding feature on a face forces you *really* to look at that face, trying to choose one outstanding characteristic of a voice forces you really to listen to that voice. That, of course, is more than half the battle; you've forced yourself to concentrate, to listen, to be *originally aware.*

The characteristic you select can be anything, as is true when working with faces. It could be an accent of course, but it could also be a squeaky quality or a screechy one. Huskiness is a voice characteristic; a particularly low or high voice might grasp your attention. There are gravelly voices, resonant voices, soothing, smooth-as-silk, or irritating voices. There are slow talkers and fast talkers. Use anything — from a speech impediment to a staccato way of speaking to a drawl. It doesn't matter; what does matter is that you have no choice but *really* to listen, with effective, *focused* attention, in order to zero in on a characteristic.

Then, associate the person's name to the voice characteristic. If Mr. Bradshaw has a very deep voice, associate your Substitute Word for the name to *deep.* For example, you might see yourself burying millions of *brads* (small nails) very deep at the shore — *brad shore/ deep*.

If you have to use *gravelly* many times, do so. It's okay to use, say, high foreheads over and over when you're applying the system to names and faces; and it's okay to use the same characteristic for different voices. After you've thought of your picture and used the name when hearing the voice three or four times, you'll simply know the name and voice. The characteristic and the picture you used will no longer be important.

Richard Schlott admits that his secretary usually tells him who's on the phone. But, he adds, "I do occasionally pick up myself. Someone who's giving us millions of dollars worth of business expects to be recognized. I'd better fit name to voice." And **Peter Kougasian** makes it a habit to "pick up my own phone calls. It is *very* important for me to know who the voice belongs to."

Richard Roth, Jr.: I'd be pretty embarrassed, and might conceivably lose business, if the person on the phone is the one who controls the money that will pay for the designing and building of a skyscraper and I don't recognize him or her instantly.

Ruth Mass: It's very important to remember the name that goes with a voice. And it'd be wonderful if that would also trigger my memory for his or her travel likes and dislikes — smoking or nonsmoking, aisle or window seat, won't stay above the seventh floor of a hotel, which airline is preferred, corporate affiliation, secretary's name.

As a matter of fact, at Ruth's firm, a "profile card" is filled out for each new client. That card contains at the head of the page information such as name, title, affiliation, address, telephone number, spouse's name, and secretary's name. You already know how to Link that kind of information.

Let's consider the association of only name to travel likes and dislikes for a moment. Ms. Levine prefers to travel first-class, in an aisle seat, nonsmoking. She's a vegetarian. She's a member of the Admirals Club (American Airlines), and her AAdvantage number is

7739485. When a rental car is needed, she prefers a Hertz car. She will not stay higher than the seventh floor in a hotel.

That's basic information; many other details may be, and usually are, included. It's easy to Link the information. Start with the Substitute Word for the name, of course. *The vine* (Levine) would do it. You can see a large vine growing over the *first-class* cabin. Visualize *only* aisle seats in that cabin — no window seats; strange-looking plane. (You can see an *isle* [with palm tree] in the cabin, if you'd rather.) Smoke billows around that single line of aisle seats — the seats frantically wave it away (nonsmoking).

See smoke billowing out of hundreds of huge vegetables (vegetarian). A gigantic vegetable is on a large ship — being the *admiral*. A large ship and the admiral fly millions of American flags (American Airlines). From a gigantic flag, you see a **cucumber fall** (AAdvantage number 7739485). If you think it's necessary, you can see a cushion on the ground — the cucumber takes *advantage* of that, and twists during its fall to land on that cushion. (You'd probably know that the number is the AAdvantage number, so it isn't really necessary to include a reminder for it — but it can't hurt!) The cucumber falls — it *hurts* (Hertz). Final picture: someone tries to climb over (higher than) a cow (7th floor); she can't — it *hurts*.

Review that Link mentally two or three times and you've *got* it. Not only do you "have" the voice and the name that goes with it, but, if you've associated the other bits of information to name (and voice), the floodgates automatically open and all those bits of information come rushing in — you simply *know* them.

HL: What would bring an employee to your attention, Mike (assuming that that might result in his or her promotion)?

Michael K. Stanton *(Partner, Weil, Gotshal and Manges, among the top twenty U.S. law firms):* Innovative thinking, effective communication, writing ability, motivation, reliability. And memory is needed in *all* those areas. One certainly can't be reliable if one doesn't remember what he has to do or where he has to be.

HL: Most executives have great memories, but it's taken for granted. They themselves don't realize it, nor how important it is.

MKS: Well, I know it's critical for the entire operation. I don't need people saying, "I'll look in the file," for everything; I can do that myself. It would be great if I always could get the answer I want or need immediately. Time is money.

24

Memory
and Management

Most aspects of managing depend on and revolve around
memory. I asked every executive I interviewed to give me
his or her thoughts on managing people. *All* of them
mentioned *showing confidence* in employees in almost all management
situations. Also mentioned by all: building employees' self-esteem,
expressing personal appreciation, pinpointing the business problem
rather than blaming the employee, asking for and showing interest in
employees' opinions and feelings. One way to show confidence in an
employee, of course, is to reinforce the good things that person has
accomplished in the past. You can say things like, "Take care of that
the way you did with ABC Corporation six years ago — that was

terrific. I know you can do it again.'' (You *remembered* what that person had done six years ago to solve the ABC Corporation problem.)

Scott Marcus: I have a very good memory. I believe that helps me to be a good executive and a good manager. I believe I could be a good executive/manager in *any* business because of my good memory. It's obvious to me. A functioning executive must remember what happened before, must be able to answer questions asked by people under him. He has to be looked up to and admired for his memory and ability. Without memory there *is* no ability.

Evan R. Bell: A good manager doesn't repeat mistakes because he *remembers* them.

The lower-level employee doesn't really have to remember anything except how to handle his or her one area of responsibility properly. The good manager has to remember the basics of *every* area within his or her larger area of responsibility. That's why I find it difficult to pull apart those two magnets — management and memory.

Managing people effectively is a skill that can be acquired (just as a trained memory can). And it's obviously a useful asset in business. Understand that the craving for appreciation is one of the deepest feelings of human nature — everyone wants to be appreciated and thought of as unique. Self-interest, the desire to be important, motivates us, is at the core of human behavior. Understand, *remember,* this truth and apply it when dealing with people; it's a powerful management tool.

Yes, you can ''deal'' with people if you don't remember who they are, what their interests are, but *not* on a management level. As a manager, you must make each person under you feel important. Getting a person to think well of you is nowhere near as important as getting him to think well of himself. Pay attention to and remember facts about individuals. Make the effort to remember and use a person's name (it's his or her most prized possession!); make the effort to remember facts about his or her professional and personal life. Justice Felix Frankfurter said that ''courtesy is the lubricant of society.'' It is. And each time you're courteous to someone in the ways mentioned above, you're acknowledging that he or she matters, that you care enough to have made the effort to *remember* him or her.

Applying the memory systems I've taught you will enable you to practice listening — I mean *really* listening. There's no way to associate or Link the facts someone is giving you without pinpointing your concentration, without paying *effective attention*. And it's impossible to separate attentive listening and interest. Really listen and you may even learn something! Stop talking about your favorite subject — you. Talk about the other person *to* that person. Work at getting him to talk about himself; what he'd like to do, what he's interested in or proud of — and *remember* those things. Utilize his or her self-interest to help you increase your own power. That's an ability possessed by most successful leaders and executives.

> **Harvey Leeds:** The capable manager has to remember to whom he delegated what. He has to remember to follow up on it, remember that it's something that has to be completed. If his memory fails, things can drop between the cracks — they're forgotten and don't get done.

Apply the memory systems to remember the good things an employee accomplishes. All you'd need to do is to associate his or her name, or the Substitute Word for the name, to the accomplishment, to the suggestion, to the amount of work done by that individual. Then, be sure to show appreciation. That's important. Experiments have proved that people who receive praise improve most in their work; people who receive reproof rate next, and those who receive *neither* show the least improvement. So, be sure to remember to show appreciation. It can sometimes be more important than financial rewards.

If an employee makes a mistake, don't put him down. Rather, you might say: "You're so close. You can do it. What do you think about doing so-and-so?" Again, here's an area where remembering what came before is important. It's the good manager who can suggest a solution because he remembers that that solution solved a similar problem years ago, perhaps even at a different firm.

We tend to imitate other people, particularly the boss. Remember, your behavior will induce similar behavior. Do as you want others to do, and they'll tend to follow your lead. You can't expect loyalty from friends and employees if you're not loyal yourself. And if your memory for business detail is obviously exceptional, your people will see that you place a high value on that ability. *You* have facts at your fingertips; they will attempt to imitate you. They'll also realize that the "I forgot" excuse is unacceptable.

So you can make people do what you want by *example* or by *suggestion*. The best way to guide actions is to guide *thinking*. To guide thinking, guide the other person's *wanting* by showing him how he can get what *he* wants. Give him the motivation that gets your ideas working in his mind. Then he'll do what you want him to do because it's what *he* wants, too!

Thinking of the other person can lead to *your* success. I remember asking a man who earned over a million dollars a year what had led to his success. He instantly replied, "Caring for other people." When he started out, he wasn't thinking of his own success as much as his *clients'* success. Helping them become successful automatically brought him success, too.

With few exceptions, most of the successful people I know (including most of those I interviewed for this book and myself as well) became successful that way — by sincerely trying to help others be successful, and remembering their likes, dislikes, and idiosyncrasies. The idea may seem obvious to you, yet it's amazing that many ambitious people, eager to climb the ladder of success, do not think of it. They probably won't make it, because looking out for the other person is often the best way to climb to the top yourself.

But, hey, let's be honest. The most marvelous, tried and true methods aren't *always* best. In the memory area — sure, occasionally just *write it down,* as I do — occasionally. And sometimes diplomacy and tact won't work. Years ago, I did appearances at an industrial show. An American corporation brought planeloads of people to a hotel near Caracas, Venezuela. Each group stayed for three days. I was the keynote speaker for each group on the night of arrival.

A young lady sang two songs, then introduced me. A company executive, Vincent Walsinski (not his real name) was entertainment chairman. I had told him that I wouldn't start until waiters were off the floor.

The first night the meal was served and concluded. Vincent asked the captain of waiters to clear the floor. The captain said that *cookies* still had to be served. Well, a large tray of cookies was served to each table — and it took *over an hour*. The show couldn't start until all the cookies were served.

This was not good. The singer, who was really an actress, got progressively more nervous. The people were tired. Vincent was annoyed. He told the captain to serve the cookies faster, or not at all. The captain said okay. The next night — no change. It took over an hour to serve the cookies. Vincent was angry.

He spent fifteen minutes telling the captain to put the cookie trays on the table before dinner, or to forget about them. He was assured that it would be taken care of. Next time, it still took over an hour to serve the cookies! Vincent was *very* angry.

He sat down with the captain and calmly (outwardly) applied all the dealing-with-people methods he knew. The captain gave his word that the situation would definitely be straightened out on the next show night. Need I tell you? That night nothing changed; Vincent trembled with rage.

He applied a nonfail method, or solution. Vincent was about five feet, eight inches tall, stocky and strong. The captain stood over six feet. I saw Vincent grab the captain's entire shirt front in one hand. He lifted him off the floor and slammed him against a wall. Nose up to nose, he *roared:* "If you serve cookies tomorrow night, I'll kill you! Understand? Serve *one* cookie tomorrow, and I'll kill you with my bare hands."

The next night the show started at a reasonable hour — no cookies were served! Vincent had found the correct method of dealing with people for this particular emergency.

(The nervous singer in this true story was Valerie Harper. You know her today as Rhoda of *The Mary Tyler Moore Show,* and then as the star of her own television show, *Valerie.*)

HL: Peter, what's important for you to remember?

Peter Kougasian *(Assistant District Attorney and Director of Legal Staff Training, Manhattan, New York):* Oh, so many things. I'm primarily a trial attorney. In court, I need to remember the facts and the law. It's nice to have documents and briefs, but it isn't effective to have to go through hundreds of pieces of paper to make the point. It takes too long; the opposing attorney can make several points in the interim.

A jury wants to believe that you are in complete control of the case. Your credibility with that jury is much higher if they see you remember all the facts. It can also make a good impression on the judge. If the judge thinks it's fresh in your mind, that can make a big difference — to your benefit. It is most effective if you can immediately state a precedent; no hesitation, just say it — know it.

25

Law, Tax, and Insurance

---

*Remember Important Information as You Read
in a Fraction of the Time It Now Takes —
Precedents, Law Section and
Internal Revenue Code Numbers, and More*

HL: So you're telling me that memory is of utmost importance to you; that you'd better remember when you're in front of a judge and jury.

Peter Kougasian: Without question. An example is citing statutes. When the legislature passes a law it is fitted into a series of books and assigned a number by which the law is cited. For instance, the statute defining disorderly conduct is penal-law section 240.20. Any lawyer handling criminal cases should know that.

The first use I made of your memory systems, Harry, as a new lawyer, was to learn the statutes and their numbers by turning the numbers into mental pictures. In a courtroom, the judge or lawyers will often refer to a statute merely by its number. The judge might

ask, "Are you adding a count of 240.20?" It wouldn't do if I had
to shuffle pages in order to know that the judge was asking if I'm
adding a disorderly conduct charge onto the other charges.

It works vice versa, too. The lawyer would say the penal-law
section number instead of reading the entire law. Saying it that
way says it all, because every judge, of course, also remembers the
statute numbers and subdivisions.

Also, it's important for me to make eye contact with the judge,
to "read" him or her. And I can't do that if I'm looking down at
documents.

Michael K. Stanton: I'm at trial mostly with corporate, commer-
cial cases. Would the judge be impressed if I stated the facts of the
case without looking at documents? Yes, yes, yes — he certainly
would be. He has to think, "This guy cares about the case, he
cares about his client, and he's fully prepared — ready to go. He
knows what he's talking about. Also — and this is important — if
you're looking down at documents, you can't "read" the judge.
It's important for me to *see* how he's reacting. Then, if I see that
the line I'm taking is turning him off, I can move to a different line;
I'll find a better time to jump back to that first line of questioning.

HL: So a lawyer in a trial situation who reads every word is not
going to be as good as the lawyer who *remembers/knows* the facts
and doesn't have to read?

MKS: Not in my judgment. He might be good, but certainly not
as effective. If you define memory as knowing the facts of a case,
on a scale of 1 to 10, I'd score memory 10. It's that critical.

Peter Kougasian mentioned that disorderly conduct is penal-law
section 240.20. To remember that just associate **nears nose**, **Nero's
nose**, **nurse nice**, or anything that phonetically *means* 240.20 to
disorderly conduct. (Nero's nose is being disorderly!)

Another example: The statute defining murder in the second degree
is 125.25. Visualize someone committing murder in the second degree
with a gigantic **toenail** and a regular *nail* to remind yourself of that. If
you need a subdivision number, simply put the Peg Word for that (*tie,
Noah, ma,* et cetera) into the picture. If the subdivision means, say,

"killing with intent" (subdivision 1), *see* that; if it means "wanton killing" (subdivision 2), see that, and so on. You'd know that the page number is 396 if you put **ambush** into the picture also.

Peter Kougasian: To be a good lawyer you have to be memorizing laws constantly, old ones and new ones. It's ineffective to say to a judge that you have a case number, a precedent, upstairs — but "I forgot the name." That doesn't make points. An example of a precedent I memorized — a great old case: *Johnson vs. Lutz*. It's a precedent regarding introduction of business records, which would ordinarily be hearsay. It's most important to remember the name of the case, but how much better also to remember the volume number, page number, the court in which it was decided, and the year. If you can cite all that it can't help but make a favorable impression on the judge.

I memorize things like this as I'm doing research, using your systems. Simple thing; but it makes legal research so much easier — and faster. It saves trips to the law books, and so on.

Oh, you may be interested in the story about a very famous lawyer — one who was *legendary* for his "photographic" memory. Something would come up during an argument, and he'd say something like, "Oh yes, if you'll notice, on page 389 of the transcript (this is during an appeal, where a transcript of the lower court trial is in use) it says such-and-such, and I'm glad you raised that point, Your Honor, because on page 592 it says such-and-such," et cetera. And, are you ready for this? *He was bluffing!* He felt that citing page numbers was that important.

HL: He got away with it for a *long* time, didn't he?

PK: Yes. My friend, the one who told me this, finally caught him. He asked the court to turn to the page this famous lawyer quoted — and they found he was bluffing. But he did get away with it for years.

If I wanted to remember the *Johnson vs. Lutz* precedent, I'd see a gigantic *john* (toilet) and its *son* introducing a large *record* (album) to empty *lots* (Lutz) at a *business* meeting. In one of those empty lots is a **new lamb** (volume 253) standing on the Empire State Building (New

York — Court of Appeals) having **dinner** (page 124). The dinner is a **mouse** (30 — 1930). I'd know that 30 meant **19**30, not 1830. If I didn't think I'd know that, I'd stick a **tub** into the picture. Again, bear in mind that you can *see* this silly picture (or pictures) in a fraction of the time it takes for me to write it, or for you to read it.

I'll anticipate a question. You do *not* have to associate this kind of information in the *same order* each time; that is, you'll *know* which association represents which piece of information.

Peter "saw" an official-looking person in his official capacity (a judge banging his gavel) being sued (handed a summons) in a **cave** — to remember that Article *78* covers the suing of an official person over an official action. (As when, in a recent case, a judge closed a trial to the public and the news media sued to have it opened again.)

"Do" a picture in your mind of, with, or between *ma berry* (Marbury) and *mad at son* (Madison) and *tie* (1) and *crunch* or *ranch* and **atomic** (137) and **dove sum** (1803) to help you know that the famous case (William) *Marbury vs.* (James) *Madison* is in the first (1) volume of the Cranch reporter at page 137. The year — 1803. A lawyer knows just what I'm talking about, and would say it, "Marbury versus Madison, one Cranch one thirty-seven, eighteen oh three." He'd be able to say it this way without looking at documents if he'd made the associations or the Link I've suggested.

In his capacity as an attorney and CPA, **Gerald S. Deutsch** deals with important clients. He told me, "It's very impressive to people attending a meeting with me for me to be able to spout from memory sections of the Internal Revenue Code, tax regulations, or both."

It's impressive and it's easy. Tax code section 274 has to do with the keeping of records for business entertainment. See a **new car** (or **Niagara**) entertaining a business acquaintance. That's all. Number 274(n) is the new law that allows only 80 percent of business entertainment to be deducted. A hu**ngry** *hen* represents 274(n); associate that to 80 percent (*fuse, fez, fuss, vase*) deduction (*D duck,* or *D duck shun* — if you need a reminder for that).

Section 267 of the Internal Revenue Code discusses disallowances of losses between related parties. (You can't sell stock at a loss to your spouse or to your own corporation and then deduct that loss.) See yourself selling something to a relation but you will accept **no check**.

Picture a **raven** owning two entities (property under each wing, perhaps) and a large hand moving parts of one entity to the other, and vice versa. This will help you remember that section 482 states that if there are two entities controlled by the same taxpaying corporation the government (large hand!), under certain circumstances, can allocate income or expenses from one to the other. Again, these are the pictures *I'd* see; you'd see the ones *you* thought of, which locks in that information. **Annul** (or **annual**) **sum** *sea* to trusting a minor (or miner or mynah bird) would tell you that *trust for a minor* is discussed in section 2503(c).

I was asked to teach a group of insurance agents how to memorize the premiums for the new term insurance policies the company was offering. The yearly premiums were different for $100,000 and $250,000 policies; they also varied, of course, for different ages and for males and females within those age limits. The chart looked something like this (I've shortened it and made up the amounts — you probably won't find policies this cheap):

Age	$100,000		$250,000	
	Male	Female	Male	Female
25	$ 85.00	$ 83.00	$175.00	$170.00
30	90.00	84.00	180.00	173.00
35	95.00	88.00	182.00	179.00
40	117.00	105.00	223.00	194.00

The agents learned the Phonetic Number/Alphabet and how to form associations in order to Link one piece of information to another. Since they *knew* that these premiums were for $100,000 and $250,000 policies, those numbers didn't have to be part of the associations. What I taught them to do was to start each short Link (or picture) with the Peg Word that represents the age — and to go from there. There are, as usual, many ways to go. Quick examples: A gigantic *nail* (25) is covered with **foil** (85) and **foam** (83); the foam oozes off the nail to tickle (175) some **ducks** or **tacks** (170). Are you with me? See the pictures, make the associations, and you'll know the premiums for a male or female up to age 25.

A *mouse* (30) is driving a **bus**; a bus is covered with **fur**; millions of **doves** are wearing fur coats: someone comes to take the furs — the doves shout, ''**Take 'em**.''

A *mule* (35) rings a **bell** with a **fife** while sitting on a **divan** (or while **divin'**) holding a **teacup**. This is an example of a ''story'' Link. You may use it, but I'd prefer: mule to bell, bell to fife, a gigantic fife is divin' (into a pool), a teacup is divin' into a pool.

A *rose* (40) has a **toothache**, a gigantic tooth twirls a **tassel**, a tassel has **no name** (you can ''see'' it saying so, or it's wearing a blank name tag), a gigantic **diaper** has no name. (For 223, you could also have ''seen'' a tassel being overlooked, and shouting ''**No no, me!**'' The same for the diaper.)

The people I talked to in these business areas — law, tax, insurance — couldn't stop expounding on how much data there is to remember within those fields. The point all of them stressed was the *expanding* and *changing* nature of the information. There are *so* many more law precedents to remember now than there were years ago; tax laws are continually changing (as, of course, you know), and so are insurance premiums and coverages. The amount of data in each area is **vast.** But that's when my systems *shine!* If there was only *a bit* of information to know, you'd eventually know it (so would everyone else in that field; you wouldn't stand out), and that'd be that. It's when the amount of data is vast, and changing, that you *need* a trained memory. Apply the systems and you have the opportunity to stand out, be noticed, and make a strong impression — gain that critical edge!

Dr. Jesse Manlapaz *(Neurosurgeon, Danbury Hospital, Danbury, Connecticut):* If I had the gift of a great memory, how would I apply it? Well, I'd certainly remember everything that ever occurred while I was doing brain surgery, and what I did to stop it, correct it, use it. There's no substitute for experience — and remembering everything that occurs becomes that body of knowledge *called* experience.

And it's quite essential to remember information I read in medical journals. It'd be great if I could read about a new drug and, as I read, remember the trade name, generic name, manufacturer, indication [what it's used for], and side effects, if any.

26

Medicine
and Related Fields

*Rx for Remembering "Trade/Generic" Names,
Journal Articles, and Other Medical Information*

Every doctor I spoke to mentioned the importance of remembering
drugs — trade and generic names, what they're for, and so on.
(One doctor said, "It's important to remember new drugs for
two reasons — for your work, of course, and so as not to look the fool
to a patient who has heard of a new drug when you haven't, or have
and have *forgotten* it!") Pharmacists have a book that lists most of the
trade/generic names. But every pharmacist I spoke to told me that
remembering them would save lots of time. When a doctor writes a
prescription for a generic drug, he doesn't necessarily have to know
that generic name. He may write the trade name and then simply write
"gen" or "generic" next to it; or he doesn't put a check in the box on

his prescription blank marked DAW — dispense as written. The pharmacist must know what the generic name of that drug is.

It should be obvious to you that all you have to do, basically, to remember these things is apply the Substitute Word System plus association. A doctor showed me the following information and wanted to see if I could remember it in one reading (or *hearing*). I did, of course, as I read it. So can you.

Mevacor is an anticholesterol drug manufactured by Merck and Company. Its generic name is lovastatin. Lifelong use of the drug may cause cataracts or liver problems for some people.

The first thing I did was to see myself calling to a large chunk of coal, saying, "Hey, *coal, let's roll*," as if we had work to do and I wanted to get it done. It sounds enough like cholesterol, certainly, to remind me of it. Of course, I know it's *anti,* not pro. If I didn't, I could have put *auntie* into that picture.

The work we had to do was to move a gigantic apple core — *move a core* to remind me of Mevacor. An enormous apple core is moved through *murky* (Merck) weather. My lover is walking through murky weather, and I call to her, *"Lover, stay thin"* — lovastatin. (*Low vest o' tin* would also do.) Lover to *cat oar acts* to *liver* (the organ, or one who lives, or *leave her*) reminds me of the possible side effects.

Sinequan is the trade name of a drug manufactured by Pfizer, Inc. The generic name is doxepin, and it is used as maintenance therapy for depression. Drowsiness is the usual side effect; it can also cause dry mouth and blurred vision, among other things. All easy to remember if you associate *cynic wan* (or *sin nick won*) to *visor* or *wiser* (Pfizer) to *docks a pin* (or *doc see pin*) to *the press* to drowsiness, and so on. Try it; see for yourself.

Valium is a trade name — associate *valley* or *valiant* to *die ace a pan* (or a girl named *Pam,* or *palm*) to remember that the generic name is diazepam. Associate Dolobid (*dole a bid* or *bed,* or *dollar bid*) to the generic name diflunisal (*dive loon is all*). Rolcatrol (*roll, cat, roll* or *roll control*) is the trade name of another drug; calcitriol (*calls it real* or *call sitter he old*) is the generic equivalent. Mephyton (*me have a ton, me fittin'*, or *me feet on*) is a trade name; the generic name is phytonadione (*fight on a Dionne, fightin' a Dionne, fittin' a Dionne,* or *fittin' a dye own*). (As I've told you, the older you get, the more you know, which means that you have more ammunition to help you form Substitute Words. If you aren't old enough to remember the Dionne quintuplets, you wouldn't have that to use as I did in this example. But a younger person might have visualized pop singer Dionne Warwick.)

Remember, the slight effort involved in thinking up Substitute Words plus forming a silly picture between two of them *traps that fleeting thought* for you.

Again, it's what comes to *your* mind for any component that's the best Substitute Word for you to use. Usually the *first* thing that comes to mind will work best. If *you* thought of it, it will remind you of what you *want* it to remind you of — instantly. For example, I used *cat oar acts* as the Substitute Word for cataracts because that's something everyone can understand. But if you visualized a person who couldn't see too well because that's what came to *your* mind as you read, that would certainly remind you of cataracts. The same would be true if you visualized a person *you* knew who is suffering from cataracts. It's an individual thing. Someone else may have thought of *cut her axe* — fine. It doesn't matter. What matters is that it reminds *you* of the piece of information. And, as you continue to apply the idea, it gets easier and easier.

> **HL:** Sheldon, are you equating being considered an authority in a field to remembering everything in that field?
> **Dr. Sheldon Lippman:** Sure. And the Specialty Board tests you on your ability to remember. After graduation, residency, you can practice pediatrics, that could be your specialty. But to get the recognition of your colleagues, you take your Specialty Board — the Board of Pediatrics. The first part is a written exam and, after a few years, you're given an oral exam. You're being tested on your knowledge in that field — they're testing your *memory.* It's prestigious, professional recognition, to pass your Specialty Board to become a Fellow of the American Academy of Pediatrics.

HL: Boils down to being a memory problem, doesn't it?

SL: Without question. And when you're recognized by the Academy, you have to recertify yourself every six years. You may be asked about areas outside your specialty. Boy, do you ever need a good memory! Extremely important.

Dr. Lippman delivered a ten-minute talk in front of his peers. Here are the highlights of that talk. Obviously, each fact reminded him of other details, since he'd studied the information in order to speak intelligently about it. He basically knew what he was talking about — he just needed a synopsis, he needed reminders.

Moyamoya is a disease that was discovered in Japan. The name means "puff of smoke." The test used to locate the disease is angiography. It's a brain X-ray using dye injection to make the blood vessels visible. When the disease exists, the blood vessels look like a puff of smoke.

It's a children's disease whose symptoms imitate seizures, like little strokes. Other symptoms are weakness on one side of the body, and losing touch with reality — like gazing into space. The wrong tests can make it seem like a neuromuscular degenerative disease — multiple sclerosis, for instance — rather than the vascular disease it is. One child had the symptoms three times before she was given the angiogram test. Then it was correctly diagnosed as moyamoya. The neurologist hadn't seen a case in fifteen years; it's that rare. The definitive treatment is surgical (grafting); drugs are used to prevent seizure and spasm.

What follows is what I'd use to remember this short talk. See yourself walking through a gigantic *puff of smoke* in Japan. You can't breathe, so you shout, *"More air, more air."* This *tells* you the name of the disease, that it was discovered in Japan, and means "puff of smoke" in Japanese. Associate *Ann gee ogre fee* or *hen geography* (angiography) to more air. Perhaps Ann needs more air and, gee, an ogre gives her some for a fee. You can *see* (X-ray) the blood vessels in an ogre's brain.

The blood vessels (you can visualize ships) sail over some children (children's disease) who seem to be having seizures or small strokes — all on one side. They all gaze into space. *Nero* (see a man playing the fiddle in a fire — Nero fiddled while Rome burned!) is *muscular* (neuromuscular). Many (multiple) see-through (clear) O's have sisters who are muscular (*multiple clear O sis* — multiple sclerosis). Some *fast cool air* (vascular) blows over the sisters; they say, "That's the real thing" (it is a vascular disease).

A child's *ma* (three times) is named Ann; she says "gee" as she gets a telegram (*Ann gee a gram*) that says "moyamoya" (the angiogram correctly diagnosed the illness as moyamoya). See the telegram using a *towel* (15) on a stethoscope (doctor). (The neurologist hadn't seen a case of moyamoya in fifteen years.)

The stethoscope is performing surgery; it is having a seizure, a spasm. Drugs pour over it and relieve the seizure/spasm.

That would do it. For me. Remember, you may select different words, different pictures, and that's just as it should be. Another way to go would be to Link the following *key* words: more air, puff, Japan, Ann gee ogre fee, brain/X-ray, children, strokes, one side, space (or gaze), Nero muscular, fast cool air, ma (if you want to be reminded that one child had the symptom *three* times), Ann gee a gram, towel, surgery/drugs.

This Link would tell you the *sequence of thoughts* that make up your talk. The more familiar with the material you are, the less components you'll need within the Link.

My rationale for using these medical examples — and all the eclectic examples in this book — should be obvious. It's important for you to realize that my memory systems may be effectively applied to *any* kind of data, in *any* business or profession.

27

Last Word

Memory is the stepping-stone to thinking.
There can hardly be one without the other.
Without memory, all intelligence and learning are lost.

There is no question that my memory systems work. Work they *have* (for many years); work they *do* (for literally millions of people, in all walks of life); work they *must* (since you tried them as you read, you *know* that). Not only does the method work, but it is the only art/skill I know that shows results immediately, *as* you're learning! And it's the only approach I know that betters you in a vital area even if it *doesn't* work.

So the question isn't whether or not the systems work, the question is how much do you want them to do for *you?* If you haven't actually tried them (and I refuse to believe that), you still don't realize how powerful, fascinating, imaginative, important, and *efficient* they are.

The incredible weapon is there; all you have to do is pick it up, cock it, *use* it.

Oh, yes, *some* effort is needed to pick it up. Tell me how many times you've acquired something valuable without applying at least a bit of effort? *Nothing* worthwhile comes easily. Let's face it, if I could put my systems in a bottle, *everyone* would have a great memory! And yet, that's almost what I've done — you're holding the bottle in your hand. Uncork it, for heaven's sake!

Of course I realize that not all the examples I've used apply directly to your particular problems. Please understand that the *concept* taught in each example most likely does. If I've made it clear that once you know the three basic ideas — Link, Peg (Phonetic Number/Alphabet) and Substitute Word — just a bit of imagination, a bit of a change or twist, can enable you to apply them to, *solve,* any business-related memory problem, then I've accomplished my purpose.

What *you* have to do is use the techniques you've learned to accomplish *your* purpose. If the title *Memory Makes Money* had anything at all to do with the fact that you picked up this book, then your purpose is clear: you want to make (more) money. Well then, use the techniques you've learned as recommended — by me and by the top-level executives who spoke to you through me — to forge ahead in business, to acquire that keen business edge that will set you apart from all the others, all the others who *don't* have the fantastic memory you now do. Your memory is ready to make money for you!

No one I have ever spoken to has questioned the importance of memory. Even the ancients knew its value. Witness this quote from a fragment of Greek writing known as *Dialexeis* that the experts date back to about 400 BC: "A great and beautiful invention is the art of memory, always useful both for learning and for life."

And, I'd add, for business.

— **HARRY LORAYNE**

Here's just a sampling of the corporations and other organizations whose headquarters or divisions (or both) use Harry Lorayne's memory systems as an ongoing part of their training programs:

Exxon Corporation; Phelps Dodge, Inc.; Metropolitan Life Insurance Company; NCR Corporation; NASA Headquarters; Texas Instruments, Inc.; IBM; Singer Company; McDonnell Douglas Corporation; Safeway Stores, Inc.; Mack Trucks, Inc.; Bendix Corporation; Indiana Bell Telephone Company; GTE Products Corporation; Bank of Nova Scotia; Wang Laboratories, Inc.; Hughes Helicopters; General Motors Corporation; Litton Systems Canada, Limited; ARCO Oil and Gas Company; Keebler Company; Morgan Guarantee Trust Company of New York; Standard Oil Company (Ohio); Martin Marietta Corporation; Boeing Computer Services Company; Chevron Corporation; Prudential Insurance Company of America; AT&T Long Lines Department; General Mills, Inc.; Irving Trust Company; Westinghouse Electric Corporation; Allied Chemical Corporation; Nestlé Company, Inc.; Bell Telephone Laboratories; Grumman Aerospace Corporation; Superior Oil Company; Stouffer's; Hartford Insurance Group; Pratt & Whitney; International Paper Company; A. C. Nielsen Company of Canada; DuPont Canada, Inc.; United States Automobile Association; Celanese Fibers Operations; Illinois Central Gulf Railroad — and more.